Reducing Your
Chapter 13 Payments:

Insider Tips and Secret Strategies!

Darrin Buggs

Legal Disclaimer

Content provided in this book is for informational purposes only and does not constitute legal advice. I am not an attorney, and the content should not be relied upon as a substitute for professional legal counsel. Always consult with a qualified legal professional for any legal concerns.

ISBN 979-8-9950062-1-3

Printed in the United States of America

DEDICATION

This book is dedicated to my grandfather, Charles Henry Cole, Sr., whose influence inspired my journey into bankruptcy law and legal writing. He taught me that education is a lifelong pursuit and that with determination, anything is possible—including the writing of this book, ***Reducing Your Chapter 13 Payments: Insider Tips and Secret Strategies!***

ABOUT THE AUTHOR

My journey into the legal field began in 2006, with my first job as a bankruptcy paralegal, where I quickly developed a strong desire to help people burdened by debt. Over the years, I worked for several renowned bankruptcy firms, each experience deepening my commitment to easing the financial struggles of my clients.

One common thread among the clients I encountered was their frustration with Chapter 13 payments. Many found these payments overwhelming, leaving them with little to no money to cover basic living expenses. I became determined to find a way to help them manage this financial burden.

To enhance my expertise, I attended Everest College for Paralegal Studies, where I gained a solid foundation in bankruptcy law. This education, combined with my hands-on experience and collaborations with seasoned attorneys, allowed me to assist my clients more effectively.

As I worked on different cases, I began to notice subtle but important ways to reduce the financial strain on my clients. Over time, as I sifted through countless legal documents, I uncovered a pattern in how Chapter 13 payments were calculated. By understanding details like allowable expenses, debt classification, and more, I discovered legitimate methods to help clients lower their monthly payments.

This discovery wasn't about exploiting loopholes—it was about using the system's rules to genuinely assist people in need. Seeing how these strategies transformed my clients' lives, I decided to compile them into a book. My hope is that this book will serve as a guide for anyone struggling to make their Chapter 13 payments.

—Darrin Buggs, *Former Senior Bankruptcy Paralegal*

Contents

Chapter 1

Chapter 13 Process: A Brief Step-by-Step Guide

The Chapter 13 process revolves around one key component—***the repayment plan***. Think of it as the *LeBron James* of Chapter 13 bankruptcy: the star player, the driving force, the essential element that makes everything work.

This plan, also known as a *reorganization plan*, gives a debtor with steady income a structured way to manage debt. It allows the debtor to reorganize what he owes to creditors in a controlled, court-supervised manner.

But how does it all come together? What steps must you take, and what should you expect along the way?

In this chapter, we'll break down the Chapter 13 process step by step. From filing your case to making payments,

and ultimately receiving a fresh start, we'll guide you through each stage so you can navigate the process with confidence.

Let's dive in.

Structuring the Chapter 13 Plan

Creating a Chapter 13 bankruptcy plan is like piecing together a complex puzzle—each step builds toward a comprehensive strategy for debt repayment and long-term financial stability. Here's how the process works:

Preparation and Counseling

Your journey begins with a mandatory credit counseling course from an approved agency. This step is more than just a requirement—it's your chance to explore alternatives to bankruptcy and gain valuable financial insight.

The counseling session must be completed within 180 days before filing. If you file your case without completing the course, you're going nowhere—your case will hit a dead end and be dismissed.

Filing the Petition

Once you've completed credit counseling, you're ready to file your bankruptcy petition. Filing includes submitting a detailed package of documents that outline your financial situation. These documents form the foundation of your Chapter 13 plan:

- **Voluntary Petition**
  The main form that officially begins your bankruptcy case.
- **Schedules of Assets and Liabilities:**

    - **Schedule A/B:** Your real and personal property
    - **Schedule D:** Secured creditors
    - **Schedule E/F:** Unsecured creditors
    - **Schedule G:** Executory contracts and leases
    - **Schedule H:** Codebtors
    - **Schedule I:** Monthly income
    - **Schedule J:** Monthly expenses

- **Statement of Financial Affairs**
  A detailed breakdown of your financial history.

- **Form 122C-1**
  Calculates your current monthly income and your applicable commitment period.

- **Form 122C-2**
  Calculates your disposable income for Chapter 13.

- **Chapter 13 Plan**
  Your proposed repayment plan.

- **Credit Counseling Certificate**
  Proof you completed the counseling session.

- **Pay Stubs / Income Evidence**
  Income documentation from the 60 days before filing.

- **Statement of Monthly Net Income**

- **Statement of Anticipated Changes in Income or Expenses**

These documents give the court, trustee, and creditors a clear picture of your finances, ensuring transparency throughout the process.

Means Test

To qualify for Chapter 13, you must pass the means test. This determines whether you have enough *disposable income* to repay a portion of your debts.

How the Means Test Works

1. **Calculate Your Average Monthly Income**
   Add all income from the past six months and divide by six.

2. **Compare to the State Median Income**
   - If you're **below** the median → you pass.

- o   If you're **above** the median → move to the next step.

3. **Deduct Allowable Expenses**

   These include housing, utilities, taxes, food, transportation, etc.

4. **Determine Disposable Income**

   What's left after allowable expenses.

5. **Assess Disposable Income**

   If you have disposable income available, you qualify for Chapter 13 and the court uses that figure to shape your repayment plan.

Example

- State median income: **$50,000**
- Your annualized income: **$54,000** (above median)
- Allowable expenses: **$3,800/month**
- Average monthly income: **$4,500**
- Disposable income: **$700/month**

Because your disposable income is $700, the court will use that amount to determine how much you will repay during your plan.

Drafting the Repayment Plan

Once you pass the means test, you must propose a repayment plan lasting three to five years. This plan must address three types of debt:

1. Secured Debts

Debts backed by collateral (homes, vehicles).
If you want to keep the property, you must pay these debts in full.

2. Priority Debts

Debts such as taxes, child support, and alimony.
These also must be paid in full.

3. Unsecured Debts

Credit cards, medical bills, personal loans.
These may be paid only partially depending on your disposable income.

Example

Debts:

- Mortgage: **$30,000**
- Car loan: **$10,000**
- Priority taxes: **$5,000**
- Credit cards: **$15,000**

Disposable income: **$700/month**

Step-by-step:

1. **Total Disposable Income Over 60 Months**
   $700 × 60 = **$42,000**

2. **Secured Debts**
   $30,000 (mortgage) + $10,000 (car) = **$40,000**

3. **Priority Debts**
   $5,000 (taxes)

4. **Unsecured Debts**
   Since secured + priority debts = **$45,000**, and you have only **$42,000**, unsecured creditors may receive little or nothing. Your attorney may need to adjust the plan or extend repayment on secured debts.

Example Monthly Breakdown

- Mortgage: **$667**
- Car loan: **$167**
- Taxes: **$84**
- **Total:** $918/month

Because your disposable income is $700/month, adjustments would be needed. This is why drafting the plan is often the most technical part of the process.

Meeting of Creditors (341 Meeting)

About one month after filing, you attend the 341 meeting. This is where the trustee—and any creditors who choose to attend—ask questions about your finances and proposed plan. It's usually brief, but essential for transparency.

Confirmation Hearing

The confirmation hearing is where the judge decides whether to approve your repayment plan.

Steps in the Confirmation Process

1. **Scheduling and Notice**
   Creditors are notified and may object.

2. **Trustee Review**
   The trustee examines your plan to ensure it meets legal and financial requirements.

3. **Objections**
   Creditors may object to payment amounts, feasibility, or debt classifications. You may negotiate or amend the plan.

4. **The Hearing**

   You, your attorney, the trustee, and any objecting creditors appear before the judge. This is the moment your plan is either approved or rejected.

5. **Approval Criteria**

   - o Good faith proposal
   - o Feasible payments
   - o Compliance with Bankruptcy Code
   - o Priority and secured debts paid correctly

6. **Judge's Decision**

   If approved, your plan becomes legally binding.

7. **Implementation**

   After confirmation, you must begin making timely payments to the trustee, who distributes them to creditors.

In Summary

The confirmation hearing (with exception of the TRCC) finalizes your Chapter 13 repayment strategy. Once confirmed, your plan governs your financial life for the next three to five years, unless later modified.

Chapter 2

Plan Payments
Under the Confirmed Plan

In the previous chapter, we briefly discussed how the proposed Chapter 13 plan is developed and presented to the court. We now turn our attention to one of the most important aspects of the confirmed plan—***plan payments***.

The plan payments are determined by the terms of the confirmed plan. They outline the amount, frequency, and duration of payments you will make to the Chapter 13 trustee, who in turn distributes those funds to your creditors.

The Nature of Plan Payments

Plan payments are the foundation of every Chapter 13 case. They are determined by the confirmed plan, not set arbitrarily by you or the trustee. The payment terms reflect the following:

1. your income,
2. allowable living expenses, and
3. the amounts required to satisfy secured, priority, and, when possible, unsecured debts.

Once the plan is confirmed, your responsibility becomes clear: make each scheduled payment in full and on time. Failure to do so may result in case dismissal or conversion to Chapter 7 bankruptcy, discussed later in this book.

How the Plan Payment Amount Is Determined

The payment amount is calculated during the post-petition stage but becomes official only upon plan confirmation. The court reviews several key factors before approval:

- **Disposable Income:** The portion of your income left after reasonable living expenses.
- **Duration of the Plan:** Typically, three to five years, depending on your income level and court requirements.
- **Debt Structure:** Priority debts (such as taxes and child support) must be paid in full, while secured debts are paid according to their collateral value and contract terms.

In a nutshell, ***disposable income*** becomes the ***plan base payment.*** The disposable income, figuratively speaking, is the "***parent***" of the plan payment—because the repayment plan originates from it.

As old folks say: "*If you want to know what a child will look like when they grow up, just look at the parents.*"

The same principle applies here. If you want a preview of what your monthly plan payments will look like, take a good look at your disposable income. The ***plan payment*** is essentially a ***mirror image*** of it.

Once the court confirms the plan, the payment amount is fixed unless your disposable income changes because of unexpected circumstances. Such changes may justify a plan modification, as we are about to discuss throughout this book.

Chapter 3

One Payment, Many Names

The payments you make under the confirmed plan are often referred to simply as *plan payments*. However, across court documents, trustee correspondence, and discussions among debtors, attorneys, and financial advisors, these payments are described using a variety of terms. Each term is in reference to your payments.

Such payments are often referred to by various names, such as:

1. **Chapter 13 Plan Payments:** The most common term used to describe the regular payments made under a Chapter 13 repayment plan.

2. **Trustee Payments:** Payments made to the bankruptcy trustee, who then distributes the funds to creditors.

3. **Plan Contributions:** Emphasizes the debtor's active role in contributing to the repayment plan.

4. **Monthly Payments:** Reflects the typical frequency with which payments are made.

5. **Repayment Plan Payments:** Highlights the purpose of these payments—to repay creditors in accordance with the bankruptcy plan.

6. **Reorganization Payments:** Used because Chapter 13 involves reorganizing debts rather than discharging them immediately.

7. **Court Payments:** An informal term denoting payments made under the supervision of the bankruptcy court.

8. **Scheduled Payments:** Refers to the structured and predictable schedule set by the confirmed plan.

9. **Debt Adjustment Payments:** Reflects Chapter 13's alternative name—"debt adjustment bankruptcy."

10. **Plan Payments:** A straightforward and widely accepted term referring to the payments made according to the Chapter 13 plan.

11. **Monthly Installments:** Describes the regular installment nature of the payments within the plan.

12. **Structured Payments:** Emphasizes the organized and systematic nature of the Chapter 13 payment schedule.

13. **Court-Ordered Payments:** Highlights that these payments are mandated as part of the bankruptcy court's order.

14. **Payments:** A simple, general term that can be used when the context of Chapter 13 bankruptcy is already clear. Even without modifiers, it effectively communicates the ongoing financial transactions involved.

15. **Chapter 13 Payments:** A clear and direct term connecting the payments to the specific chapter of the Bankruptcy Code.

These terms may be used interchangeably depending on the context and the practices of attorneys, trustees, and courts involved in the bankruptcy process. For clarity and consistency, throughout this book we will primarily refer to them as **"plan payments"** or simply **"payments."**

Role of the Chapter 13 Trustee: Management of Plan Payments

We've seen that **plan payments** can be described in many different ways, each reflecting a unique aspect of the debtor's financial commitment under Chapter 13 bankruptcy. No matter what these payments are called, one thing remains the same: someone must manage, track, and distribute them properly. That responsibility belongs to the **Chapter 13 trustee**.

The trustee plays a central role in ensuring that all payments are made on time, in full, and in accordance with the court-approved plan, helping guide the debtor along a structured path toward financial recovery.

As outlined in **11 U.S.C. § 1302(b)**, *"The Chapter 13 trustee both evaluates the case and serves as a disbursing agent, collecting payments from the debtor and making distributions to creditors."* This dual responsibility places the trustee at the heart of the Chapter 13 repayment system—overseeing compliance and ensuring fairness for all parties involved.

Chapter 13 plan payments are typically made monthly, with plan durations ranging from 36 to 60 months, depending on the debtor's income and total debt obligations. The trustee's involvement spans this entire period, from the first payment to the final distribution. As one paralegal humorously noted, *"The trustee is always pocket-watching the debtor."* In other words, the trustee consistently monitors the debtor's financial activity, ensuring continued adherence to the repayment plan and steady progress toward completion.

Payment Options

Debtors have several methods to make their Chapter 13 plan payments, allowing for flexibility and convenience while maintaining compliance with court requirements.

Online Payments

Most trustees now provide secure **online payment portals**, often accessible through the trustee's official website. These platforms allow debtors to make payments using credit or debit cards and to track their payment history with ease. However, it's important to note that some online systems may charge small processing fees for this service.

Mail-in Payments

Mail-in payments remain a reliable traditional option. Debtors can send checks or money orders directly to the trustee's office via the postal service. This method offers simplicity and does not require online banking access, though it's essential to allow enough time for mail delivery to avoid late payments.

Direct Deposit (ACH Transfers)

Direct deposit or **automatic withdrawals** provide convenience and consistency. By authorizing automatic transfers from a personal bank account—typically through an **Automated Clearing House (ACH) agreement)**—the debtor ensures timely, worry-free payments. This "set it and forget it" method minimizes the risk of missed payments and provides added assurance for both debtor and trustee.

Trustee Administrative Fees

The trustee plays a key role in making sure your Chapter 13 plan stays on track. And like anyone providing a professional service, the trustee is compensated for that work. This compensation comes in the form of an **administrative fee**—a small percentage deducted from each plan payment before distributions are made to creditors.

The exact fee amount **varies by jurisdiction** but is set and regulated by the U.S. Trustee Program. You do not pay this fee separately. Instead, it is built into your plan payment, meaning the trustee receives their compensation automatically as part of the normal distribution process.

Understanding how payments are managed, the available payment methods, and the trustee's role in monitoring your progress can help you stay organized and confident throughout your plan.

But sometimes, things change along the way. You might lose income, face new expenses, or experience other challenges that make your current payment plan hard to keep up with. When that happens, you may need to adjust your plan. In the next chapter, we'll talk about *plan modifications* — what they are, when you can ask for one, and how to make sure your plan still works for your situation.

Chapter 5

Plan Modification

Life can change quickly—one moment everything is fine, and the next, it's not. The same is true even after filing for Chapter 13 bankruptcy. Fortunately, the bankruptcy system recognizes this and allows for modifications to your Chapter 13 plan if significant changes occur.

Plan modification is crucial for adjusting your Chapter 13 payments. Nearly every Chapter 13 case involves the possibility of modifying the plan, which can save you a significant amount of money.

In this chapter, we'll discuss when and why you might need a modification, the legal steps involved, and the potential outcomes. By understanding the plan modification process, you can potentially lower your plan payments and better manage your financial situation.

The Bankruptcy Code

If your Chapter 13 payments are too high and you can no longer make them, you may apply for a plan modification under **11 U.S.C. § 1329** of the Bankruptcy Code. This section outlines the circumstances under which a debtor, trustee, or unsecured creditor may request a modification after the plan has been confirmed.

Key Provisions of 11 U.S.C. § 1329:

- **Who Can Request a Modification:** The debtor, the trustee, or the holder of an unsecured claim may request a modification.

- **When a Modification Can Be Requested:** A modification may be requested at any time after the plan is confirmed, but before completion of payments under the plan.

- **Types of Modifications Allowed:** The court may approve modifications that:

  1. Increase or decrease the amount of payments on claims of a particular class.

  2. Extend or shorten the time for payments.

  3. Adjust distributions to a creditor if payments were made outside the plan.

  4. Provide for payment of claims filed after initial confirmation but before the filing deadline.

- **Confirmation of Modified Plan:** The modified plan must still meet Chapter 13 requirements, including good faith, feasibility, and compliance with the Bankruptcy Code.

This section ensures that your repayment plan can be adjusted to reflect significant changes in your financial situation.

When and Why You Might Need a Modification

Life is unpredictable, and your financial circumstances may change during the three to five year Chapter 13 repayment period. You might need a modification if you experience:

1. **Income Changes:** A reduction in income due to job loss, reduced hours, or salary cuts can make it difficult to keep up with your plan. Conversely, an increase in income might allow faster repayment of debts.

2. **Unexpected Expenses:** Emergencies such as medical bills, home repairs, or other unforeseen costs can strain your budget.

3. **Changes in Living Expenses:** Rising costs for utilities, rent, or transportation may require plan adjustments.

4. **New Financial Obligations:** Major life events—marriage, the birth of a child, or supporting elderly parents—can introduce new financial responsibilities.

The Process of Modifying a Chapter 13 Plan

1. **Identify the Need for Modification:** Track your income and expenses regularly. Recognize when your current plan is no longer feasible.

2. **Consult Your Attorney:** Discuss your situation with your bankruptcy attorney, who can help determine whether a modification is necessary and feasible.

3. **Draft the Modified Plan:** With your attorney, create a revised plan that reflects your new financial circumstances, detailing changes in income, expenses, and repayment ability.

4. **File a Motion to Modify:** Submit a motion with the bankruptcy court, including the revised plan and a clear explanation of the reasons for the modification.

5. **Notify Creditors and Trustee:** Creditors and the Chapter 13 trustee are given notice of the proposed modification and may raise objections.

6. **Address Objections:** Negotiate with creditors or provide additional documentation to resolve concerns.

7. **Court Approval:** Attend a hearing where the judge evaluates whether the modification is necessary, feasible, and made in good faith.

8. **Implement the Modified Plan:** If approved, begin making payments according to the new plan. Follow it meticulously to stay compliant.

Criteria for Approval

The court considers several factors when deciding whether to approve a plan modification:

- **Good Faith:** The modification must be requested in good faith, not as an attempt to avoid paying debts.
- **Feasibility:** The modified plan must realistically reflect your ability to pay based on updated income and expenses.
- **Compliance with the Bankruptcy Code:** The plan must meet all legal requirements, including fair treatment of creditors.

Potential Outcomes of a Plan Modification

- **Adjusted Payment Amounts:** Monthly payments may decrease (or, in some cases, increase) based on your financial situation.
- **Extended or Shortened Plan Duration:** Plan length may change within the three to five year limit.
- **Altered Debt Prioritization:** Payment allocations among secured, priority, and unsecured debts may be adjusted.
- **Continued Legal Protection:** You remain protected under Chapter 13, including the automatic stay, as long as you follow the modified plan.

Example: Applying for a Plan Modification Due to Loss of Income

Suppose you are three years into your Chapter 13 plan, making your monthly payment of $1,500. Suddenly, you lose your job, reducing your income by 40%. Your current plan is no longer feasible. Here's how a modification would work:

Step 1: Recognize the Need

You notice that with your new income and unemployment benefits, you can only afford $900 per month instead of $1,500.

Step 2: Consult Your Attorney

You review your new income, savings, and budget with your attorney to determine the best course of action.

Step 3: Draft the Modified Plan

With your attorney, you draft a revised plan proposing payments of $900 per month, supported by documentation of your job loss, unemployment benefits, and revised budget.

Step 4: File a Motion to Modify

Your attorney files the motion with the court, including the modified plan and explanation of circumstances.

Step 5: Notify Creditors and Trustee

Creditors and the trustee receive notice of the modification and may object.

Step 6: Address Objections

You provide additional documentation or negotiate with creditors as needed.

Step 7: Court Approval

The judge reviews the motion, ensures good faith, feasibility, and compliance, and approves the modification, setting your new payment at $900 per month.

Step 8: Implement the Modified Plan

You begin making the reduced payments and continue following the terms of the modified plan.

Criteria in This Example:

- **Good Faith:** The request was made due to unforeseen job loss.
- **Feasibility:** Payments reflect the reduced income realistically.
- **Compliance:** The plan still treats creditors fairly and meets all legal requirements.

Section 1329 is the *primary* gateway for all debtors to modify their confirmed plan and when appropriate, reduce their plan payments, as explained in the following chapters.

Chapter 6

Extending Your Chapter 13 Plan to Reduce Monthly Payments

One of the most flexible tools built into a Chapter 13 bankruptcy is the *duration*, which is the length of time you will spend under the plan. Many debtors don't realize that adjusting the length of their plan can significantly lower their monthly payments.

Fortunately, this is a well-established and straightforward process. By extending your repayment period—within the limits allowed by law—you may be able to cut your plan payments by a substantial amount.

This chapter walks you through the rules, the mechanics, and the practical steps for extending your plan the right way.

Understanding the Statutory Limits of a Chapter 13 Plan

Every Chapter 13 plan must fit within the time limits set by the Bankruptcy Code. Under 11 U.S.C. § 1322(d), the allowable plan length—called the "applicable commitment period"—is:

- **36 months** for debtors whose income is **below** the state median, and
- **60 months** for debtors whose income is **above** the state median.

No Chapter 13 plan may exceed 60 months from the date the first payment becomes due. Think of these limits as the plan's "bookends"—they define how short or long the plan can legally run. Most plans fall somewhere between 36 and 60 months, depending on each debtor's financial situation.

How the Means Test Determines Plan Length

Your plan length is largely determined by the Means Test, which compares your **gross household income** to your state's median income for a household of your size.

- **Below-median income** → eligible for a **36-month** plan
- **Above-median income** → required to propose a **60-month** plan

Example

Sarah, a single mother of two in California, earns gross monthly income of $4,000. The median income for a household of three in her state is $5,000. Because she falls below that amount, Sarah qualifies for a 36-month plan.

Her Means Test shows $500 in monthly disposable income. Since her calculation supports it, her plan payment is set at $500 for 36 months.

This example demonstrates how the Means Test determines both the **duration** of the plan and the **starting point** for the monthly payment.

Lowering Monthly Payments by Extending the Plan

The length of your plan directly affects the size of your monthly payment. Extending the plan gives you more months to pay the same required amount, resulting in lower monthly payments—provided you stay within the 60-month legal limit.

If your confirmed plan is **less than 60 months**, you may be able to extend it and reduce your payment. If your plan is already **at 60 months**, no extension is legally allowed.

Example

- **Debtor Green** is in a 36-month plan but is struggling to afford payments. By extending the plan to 60 months, Green spreads the same repayment amount over more months, lowering the monthly payment.
- **Debtor Blue** is already in a 60-month plan. Because this is the statutory maximum, no extension is available.

As Kentucky bankruptcy attorney Andrea Wasson explains, you can often "stretch out the payments over a longer period of time in order to lower your monthly Chapter 13 plan payment." In most cases, this reduces the monthly burden without increasing the total repayment amount—though your trustee must still review the modification.

Bottom line: More months = smaller payments.

Chart: How Extending Your Plan Affects Payments

Plan Duration	Monthly Payment	Total Paid Over Life of Plan	Effect on Budget
36 months	$500	$18,000	Higher monthly burden
48 months	$375	$18,000	Moderate burden
60 months	$300	$18,000	Lowest monthly burden

Notes:

- Assumes the same total repayment amount.
- Extending the plan spreads required payments over more months.
- Shorter plans finish faster but create higher monthly obligations.

- Your actual numbers may differ depending on disposable income, secured obligations, and trustee requirements.

STEP-BY-STEP GUIDE: Extending Your Chapter 13 Plan

Use this roadmap to evaluate whether extending your plan can help lower your monthly payment.

STEP ONE — Obtain a Copy of Your Confirmed Plan

Start by gathering your documents. If you don't have a copy of your confirmed plan, request one from your attorney, the trustee, or the bankruptcy court.

Action Items:

- Locate your confirmed plan.
- Ensure it is the **court-approved** version, not a proposed or amended draft.

STEP TWO — Review the Confirmed Plan

Carefully review the plan to determine its current duration. The plan term is typically found in the introductory sections.

Action Items:

- Highlight the section that states the number of months in your plan.
- Ask your attorney to explain any unclear language.

STEP THREE — Determine Eligibility for Extension

A plan can only be extended if it is under 60 months.

If your plan is already 60 months, the Bankruptcy Code does not allow further extension.

Action Items:

- Compare your current plan length to the 60-month limit.
- The shorter your existing plan, the greater the potential payment reduction.

STEP FOUR — Contact Your Bankruptcy Attorney

Once you've confirmed your plan's length, speak with your attorney to ensure extension is the best strategy. They can evaluate whether extending the plan or using other tools—such as surrendering property or adjusting expenses—might offer greater relief.

Action Items:

- Explain your financial difficulty.
- Ask whether extending your plan is the most effective and permissible solution.

STEP FIVE — File a Plan Modification

Your attorney will prepare and file a §1329 motion to modify your plan. This modification requests to extend the plan to a new duration (up to 60 months) and recalculates your payment accordingly.

Action Items:

- Have your attorney draft and file the modification.
- Ensure the new plan clearly describes the extended term and adjusted payment.
- Serve the required parties under local rules (e.g., trustee and affected creditors).

STEP SIX — Await Court Review and Approval

Once submitted, the trustee and judge will review your modification. There may be objections or a short hearing. If approved, your plan is officially extended.

Action Items:

- Watch for notices of objection or hearing dates.
- Keep a copy of the signed order approving the modification.

STEP SEVEN — Follow the Updated Payment Schedule

When the court approves the modification, the trustee will adjust your payment schedule. You must continue making payments consistently under the new terms to stay on track for discharge.

Action Items:

- Confirm your new monthly payment with the trustee.
- Stay current to complete your extended plan successfully.

Final Note: Use the Tool Strategically

Extending your Chapter 13 plan isn't a loophole—it's a lawful, built-in mechanism designed to help debtors stay afloat and complete their case. When used strategically, this adjustment can give you the breathing room necessary to stay the course without jeopardizing your bankruptcy.

Think of it as the same song, played at a slower, steadier pace.

10 Key Points

1. Chapter 13 plans must last between 36 and 60 months under federal law.
2. Your *income level* determines whether you start with a 36 or 60 month plan.
3. Extending your plan (up to 60 months) can lower your monthly payment.
4. Plans already at 60 months *cannot* be extended.
5. The strategy only applies to plans shorter than 60 months.
6. Extending a plan with only a few months left may result in minimal savings.
7. Lower monthly payments help short-term cash flow but may lengthen the time to discharge.
8. The Means Test determines your initial plan length and payment structure.
9. The Bankruptcy Code places strict limits on how long a Chapter 13 plan can run.
10. Extending a plan typically lowers monthly payments by spreading the same repayment across more months, subject to trustee review.

Chapter 7
Surrendering Secured Property

Extending the months isn't the only tool you can use to reduce your Chapter 13 plan payments. Throughout this book, you'll discover several strategies that can help bring those payments down—especially if you own *secured property*.

Now, for those unfamiliar with the term, don't worry—we'll soon explain exactly what secured property means. Just hold your horses for a moment.

First, let's get this out of the way: eliminating or surrendering any secured property can dramatically reduce your monthly payment obligations. This method works almost like magic.

What Is Secured Property?

Secured property refers to **assets pledged as collateral** for a loan. The creditor has a legal right to repossess or sell the property if the debtor defaults. This is different from unsecured debt, which has no collateral backing it.

Common examples of secured property include:

1. **Real Estate:** Homes, land, or other mortgaged property. The lender can foreclose if payments are missed.
2. **Vehicles:** Cars, trucks, motorcycles, boats, or other financed vehicles. Lenders may repossess these assets if payments lapse.
3. **Household Items:** Less common, but appliances, furniture, or equipment can sometimes be secured.

Sidebar: Secured property is also called **secured debt** or **secured asset**. All three terms refer to the same concept: a debt backed by a specific asset.

Schedule D: Documenting Your Secured Debt

In a bankruptcy petition, **Schedule D** lists all secured debts. It's completed at the outset of the case and includes:

- **Creditor Information:** Name, address, and contact info.
- **Lien Details:** Type of lien and property used as collateral.
- **Claim Amount:** Total amount owed.
- **Collateral Description & Value:** Detailed info about the asset.
- **Unsecured Portion:** If the debt exceeds collateral value, the remainder is listed as unsecured.

Schedule D is essential because it helps the court, trustee, and creditors understand your secured obligations — which directly impacts your Chapter 13 plan and payment calculation.

The Power of Secured Debt; Using It as an Instrument to Reduce Plan Payment

One of the most effective — and often overlooked — tools is using secured debt as a lever to reduce your plan payments.

Under §1329(a) of the Bankruptcy Code, you have the right to modify your plan after confirmation. This means your repayment plan isn't locked in stone. If circumstances change, you can make adjustments — including removing secured debt that no longer works in your favor.

This legal process is known as surrendering a secured asset. It's entirely voluntary — no one can force you to keep property you no longer want or can't afford.

The Power of Surrendering

Let's put it into real-world terms. Suppose you have a vehicle listed in your plan, but the monthly payment is stretching your budget too thin. You have every right to surrender it. Maybe you're trying to lower your plan payments or simply want to move on from the asset — either way, the law supports your decision.

Even the courts recognize this as a practical strategy to lower your repayment obligation. Judge Randolph J. Haines once pointed out that debtors should look for ways to reduce expenses, such as surrendering property, rather than dismissing their entire case. In other words — don't quit, adjust.

How the Process Works

To make it official, you'll file a plan modification with your bankruptcy court. Once approved, the property goes back to the lienholder, who sells it to recover part of the debt. Any leftover balance often becomes unsecured debt, which may later be reduced or wiped out entirely through your plan.

Here's the best part: When that secured item is removed from your plan, the payments once tied to it disappear as well. This automatically lowers your overall plan payment. The effect is simple but powerful.

Whether it's a car, house, or another secured asset, surrendering it can be a strategic move for payment reduction. Just as that debt was factored into your plan at confirmation, it can be factored out — often dollar for dollar.

The results are always the same: smaller payments.

STEP-BY-STEP GUIDE: Reducing Plan Payments by Surrendering Secured Property

Before you start — quick checklist

- Talk to your attorney. (Non-negotiable.)
- Pull a copy of your confirmed plan and Schedule D.
- Gather titles, loan statements, and any vehicle/home condition info.
- Make notes on why you want to surrender the asset (reduce payment, no longer needed, etc.).

STEP ONE: CONSULT YOUR ATTORNEY

Your lawyer guides the legal steps and drafts the paperwork. If you have a paid attorney, consult them first. If you're pro se, you still should follow court rules and consider talking to local legal aid for help.

Action items:

- Explain why you want to surrender the asset.
- Ask your attorney to prepare the plan modification and any required notices.

STEP TWO: EVALUATE YOUR SECURED DEBT (Schedule D)

Review every secured item listed on Schedule D. Ask practical questions:

- Is this asset worth keeping? Is it drivable or sellable?
- Will keeping it cause you to default on the plan?
- Could surrendering it meaningfully lower your monthly payment?
- For homes: would surrender mean relocation or downsizing?

Action items:

- Mark the property you plan to surrender.
- Get payoff/loan balances and lienholder contact info.

STEP THREE: DRAFT THE PLAN MODIFICATION

Your modification should plainly state you are surrendering the identified secured property and request reclassification of any deficiency as unsecured debt (if appropriate).

What to include:

- Case caption and case number.
- Clear description of the property being surrendered (make/model, VIN, address, etc.).
- Statement that the debtor surrenders the property to the lienholder.
- Request that any remaining deficiency be treated as unsecured (if you want that result).
- Any proposed changes to plan payment amounts or allocation.

Sample line (example only):

"Debtor hereby surrenders the 2016 Ford F-150 (VIN XXXXXXXXX) to Creditor ABC Auto, and requests that any resulting deficiency be treated as unsecured under the confirmed plan."

STEP FOUR: FILE & SERVE THE MODIFICATION

File the modification with the bankruptcy court where your Chapter 13 was filed. Serve copies on the chapter 13 trustee, the affected creditor(s), and any required parties under local rules.

Action items:

- File modification with the court clerk (electronic filing if available).

- Serve the trustee and lienholder per local procedures.

- Keep proof of service.

STEP FIVE: MONITOR FOR OBJECTIONS & ATTEND HEARING IF NEEDED

After filing, the trustee or creditor may object. Be prepared for a hearing or to supply additional information.

Action items:

- Check the court docket or ask your attorney to watch for objections.
- Attend any scheduled hearing and be ready to explain why surrender is appropriate.

STEP SIX: COURT APPROVAL & EFFECT ON PAYMENTS

If the court approves the modification, the surrendered property is removed from the plan and the payments that were allocated to that secured creditor stop being required — which lowers your plan payment.

Action items:

- Obtain a copy of the court order approving the modification.
- Verify trustee recalculated payment (if applicable).
- Confirm how any deficiency is being treated (unsecured vs. paid).

STEP SEVEN: COORDINATE WITH THE LIENHOLDER

Once surrendered, the lienholder will repossess or sell the property to recover what's owed.

Action items:

- Provide lienholder with any necessary information (location of property, keys, title — follow local repossession rules).

- Keep records of communications and any sale notices.

AFTER IT'S ALL DONE — KEEP RECORDS & RECHECK YOUR PLAN

- Save the filed modification, the court order, proof of service, and all correspondence.

- Confirm your monthly plan payment on the trustee's docket or statement.

- Update your mental budget — you should see the payment relief you sought.

10 Key Points

1. Secured property is backed by collateral.
2. Secured property includes homes, vehicles, and similar assets.
3. You may choose to surrender a secured item listed in your case.
4. Surrendering secured property can effectively reduce your plan payments.
5. A plan modification is the legal process used to surrender your property.
6. Plan modifications are filed with your bankruptcy case.
7. No one can prevent you from surrendering secured property.
8. The Code grants you the right to modify your confirmed plan to remove secured properties.
9. The decision to surrender property may be based on a desire to lower your plan payments.
10. In your bankruptcy case, Schedule D lists all secured debts.

Chapter 8

Loss of Income

A debtor rushed into his attorney's office, his face full of worry. He went straight to the receptionist, asking urgently to speak with his lawyer. Even though the office didn't allow walk-ins, the receptionist made an exception and scheduled him right away.

When he finally sat down, the words came out fast: "I lost my second job," he said. "Now my bankruptcy case might get dismissed—I could lose everything."

The attorney listened calmly and reassured him that there was a solution. He explained that when income drops, your disposable income drops as well, and because disposable income is what determines your Chapter 13 plan payment, a debtor can request a plan modification to lower that payment.

Just like this debtor, you can use the same option to make your Chapter 13 plan payments much lower. This chapter will show you how to do it step by step.

Income

Income plays a central role in Chapter 13 bankruptcy. Because Chapter 13 is based on a repayment plan, a debtor must have a regular and reliable source of income to qualify. This is why a Chapter 13 debtor is often referred to as a "wage earner."

Most debtors are traditional employees who receive a W-2 each year, but self-employed individuals or small business owners can also file under Chapter 13.

In those cases, business profits can serve as the source of income for plan payments.

According to bankruptcy attorney and author Cara O'Neill, in her book *Chapter 13 Bankruptcy: Keep Your Property & Repay Debts Over Time*, explains that the following "regular income" is a foundational requirement for qualifying under Chapter 13:

- Regular wages or salary
- Self-employment income
- Seasonal or commission-based work
- Pension or retirement income
- Social Security or disability benefits
- Workers' compensation or unemployment benefits
- Welfare, child support, or alimony
- Rental income or property sale proceeds (especially when selling is part of business operations)

All income sources must be reported. If married—even if filing alone—the spouse's income must also be included. Income may also include regular contributions from relatives or household members who help pay household expenses.

Means Test

The means test determines how much a debtor can afford to pay through the Chapter 13 repayment plan. It compares the debtor's income to the state median income for a household of similar size, based on income received during the six months before filing.

Below the State Median

If your income is below your state's median income:

- You must still complete the income portion of the Chapter 13 means test (Form 122C-1).
- You are **not required** to complete the expense portion (Form 122C-2).
- Your plan mainly focuses on paying secured and priority debts (like car loans or taxes).
- Unsecured creditors may receive little or nothing.
- Your plan can last **36 months** instead of 60.

Above the State Median

If your income is above the median, you must complete the full means test to calculate your **disposable income**. This requires:

- Listing all income sources
- Applying IRS expense standards
- Ensuring secured and priority debts are fully paid
- Meeting the "best effort" requirement for unsecured creditors

If your income is above the median, your plan must usually run for **60 months** and must meet all repayment requirements for court approval.

Example: John's Chapter 13 Bankruptcy

John's Profile

- Single filer with a monthly income of $4,000
- State median income for one person: $3,500
- Debts: car loan (secured), tax debt (priority), and credit cards (unsecured)

Scenario 1: Below Median

If John earned less than $3,500:

- He would only need to complete the income portion of the forms.
- His plan would focus on secured and priority debts.
- Unsecured creditors might receive little or nothing.
- Plan length: **36 months**.

Scenario 2: Above Median

Since John earns $4,000—above the median—he must complete the full means test.

Step 2: Determining Disposable Income

- Gross monthly income: $4,000
- Allowable living expenses: $2,500
- Disposable income: $1,500

Step 3: Chapter 13 Plan

- Monthly payment to trustee: **$1,500 for 60 months**
- Pays secured, priority, and required unsecured claims
- Remaining eligible debts are discharged after plan completion

This example shows how the means test shapes both the structure and duration of a Chapter 13 repayment plan.

Disposable Income = Monthly Plan Payments

Your **disposable income** determines your **monthly plan payment**. The calculation is straightforward:

1. Calculate Gross Income

Include all income sources: wages, commissions, business profits, benefits, rental income, or retirement income.

2. Subtract Allowed Deductions

IRS National and Local Standards are used to calculate:

- Housing and utilities
- Food, clothing, transportation
- Healthcare and medical expenses
- Childcare or education
- Secured debt payments (mortgage, car loans)
- Priority debts (taxes, child support)

3. Determine Disposable Income

Income – Allowed Expenses = Disposable Income.

Once you subtract allowable expenses from your income, the remainder becomes your *disposable income*.

4. Monthly Plan Payment

Your *disposable income* becomes your *plan payment* until adjusted by secured or priority debt obligations or a loss of income.

Loss of Income: Good Cause for Plan Payment Reduction

As noted earlier, your income is the backbone of your Chapter 13 plan. Once the plan is confirmed, you are required to keep up with payments. But life happens—job loss, reduced hours, pay cuts, or loss of business can all affect your ability to stay current.

The good news: loss of income is one of the most common and well-recognized reasons courts allow a plan modification.

Bankruptcy attorney John T. Orcutt notes that it is normal for Chapter 13 debtors to experience income changes during their case. When that happens, you may request a payment reduction through either:

- An informal modification with the trustee, or
- A formal modification filed with the court

Legal research also confirms that courts routinely approve modifications when debtors suffer job loss, demotion, or other legitimate financial hardships—because these events directly affect disposable income.

When your *income* drops, your ***disposable income*** and ***trustee payments*** drop as well. The two are connected like Siamese twins—each one affecting the other. So it makes sense to expect a reduction in your ***plan payments*** when your ***disposable income*** can no longer support your financial obligations under your confirmed plan.

The key is acting quickly. Apply for a §1329 motion to lower your plan payments based on some sort of income loss. If approved, the court can modify your plan to make your payments manageable.

A loss of income does **not** have to end your bankruptcy case. With prompt action and proper modification, your plan can remain on track with Chapter 13 payments favorable to you. A big ***WIN***.

STEP-BY-STEP GUIDE: What to Do When Income Changes

STEP 1: Identify the Income Loss

Common causes include:

- Job termination or layoff
- Reduced hours or overtime
- Demotion or pay cut

- Loss of business income
- Decreased financial contributions from a household member

Understanding the cause of the loss helps your attorney build a clear explanation for the court.

STEP 2: Provide Proof of Loss of Income

Gather documentation such as:

- Recent pay stubs
- Termination or layoff letter
- Updated profit-and-loss statements
- Written statement from a contributing household member

Complete documentation is critical. Missing records can delay approval.

STEP 3: Contact Your Attorney

Notify your attorney immediately and provide all supporting documents. Early involvement helps prevent missed payments and reduces dismissal risk.

STEP 4: Request A Modification

Your attorney will either:

- Try an informal adjustment with the trustee
- Or file a formal Motion to Modify the Confirmed Plan with the court

The court can then approve a reduction in your monthly plan payments based on your current financial situation.

10 Key Points

1. During a Chapter 13 bankruptcy, a debtor may experience a loss of income.
2. Income loss can result from job loss, reduced hours, or a pay cut.
3. The loss can affect anyone whose income contributes to the household budget used to fund the plan.
4. Income is essential to the success of a Chapter 13 case.
5. The debtor must have a regular and reliable source of income to qualify.
6. Chapter 13 is often called a "wage earner's plan," but the Bankruptcy Code does not use that term.
7. After plan approval, the debtor must maintain sufficient income to continue payments.
8. To request a modified plan due to income loss, the debtor must provide documentation such as pay stubs or a termination letter.
9. Some attorneys attempt an informal adjustment with the trustee before seeking court approval.
10. A formal modification requires submitting a revised plan to the bankruptcy court for approval.

Chapter 9
Suspending Your Plan Payments

Filing your Chapter 13 case brings instant relief. Creditor calls stop, the pressure eases, and for a moment life feels calm again—almost like taking a short vacation.

But sometimes life throws another curveball. A sudden reduction in income or unexpected financial strain can leave you struggling to keep up with your monthly trustee payments.

When this happens, it's not the end of your case. Bankruptcy law allows you to request a temporary suspension of your plan payments, known as a ***moratorium***.

Unlike other tools discussed earlier—such as modifying surrendering property or extending your plan months—a moratorium does not reduce the total amount you owe under your plan. Instead, it simply pauses your payments for a short, court-approved period. Even though it doesn't lower your plan obligation, this temporary pause can ***feel like a payment reduction***, giving you relief from out-of-pocket payments for a set time while you regain financial stability.

Plan Moratorium, Defined

In bankruptcy proceedings, a Chapter 13 plan moratorium is the legal authorization that allows you to temporarily delay your required plan payments.

The Oxford English Dictionary defines a moratorium as *"a **legal authorization for debtors to postpone payment.**"*

In practical terms, a plan moratorium gives you the right to pause your payments to the trustee for a set period. At its core, it is simply a formal way of saying "suspension"—in this case, the suspension of your Chapter 13 payment obligations.

This suspension provides short-term relief by freeing you from making out-of-pocket plan payments for a limited time. During the approved pause, you can stop making payments without penalties or defaulting under your confirmed plan. For many debtors, this tool is essential during periods of financial hardship, helping manage cash flow and avoid further financial stress.

The legal authority for a plan moratorium comes from Section 1329 of the Bankruptcy Code, which allows a confirmed Chapter 13 plan to be modified after confirmation. These modifications can include temporarily suspending or adjusting payments, or extending the payment schedule within the limits set by law. This framework enables the court to provide temporary relief while ensuring the overall plan remains enforceable and structured.

Good Causes for Suspension of Payments

A Chapter 13 plan moratorium is not automatic—you must show the court that there is a legitimate reason, or "good cause," for temporarily suspending your payments. To have the best chance of approval, it is important to clearly document your circumstances and provide supporting evidence. This may include pay stubs, medical bills, repair estimates, or other records that demonstrate your financial hardship. Presenting a clear, organized case to the court helps the judge understand why a temporary suspension is necessary.

Courts generally look for circumstances that make it difficult or impossible for you to meet your plan obligations without causing undue hardship.

Here is a summary of common good causes that may justify a suspension of Chapter 13 payments:

1. **Loss of Income:** Job loss, reduction in work hours, or termination of benefits that significantly reduce income.
2. **Unanticipated Expenses:** Sudden bills or repairs, such as medical costs, car, or home repairs.
3. **Short-term Unemployment or Disability:** Temporary injury or disability that prevents working.
4. **Business Expenses:** Essential, unexpected expenses for self-employed debtors, such as equipment repair or replacement.
5. **Impending Foreclosure or Repossession:** Urgent secured debt issues requiring temporary relief.
6. **Natural Disasters or Catastrophic Events:** Events like fire, flood, or severe weather damage.
7. **Substantial Changes in Financial Circumstances:** Significant financial changes that make plan payments unaffordable.
8. **Legal or Court-Ordered Obligations:** Payments or legal expenses that strain resources.
9. **Medical Emergencies:** Health crises leading to high medical expenses.
10. **Loss of Social Security Benefits or Other Government Assistance:** Reduction or termination of benefits previously relied upon for plan payments.

Each case is unique, and the decision rests with the bankruptcy judge based on the evidence presented.

WHAT IS THE LONGEST A JUDGE WILL PERMIT SUSPENSION OF PLAN PAYMENTS?

There is **no fixed nationwide limit**. The judge decides based on:

- Your payment history
- The reason for the missed payments
- The remaining length of your plan
- Whether your proposed modification keeps the plan feasible

However, most courts approve modifications that suspend payments for 1 to 3 months, sometimes up to 6 months in cases of documented hardship (such as medical emergencies or temporary unemployment). Anything longer typically requires strong proof and trustee cooperation.

STEP-BY-STEP GUIDE: Requesting a Suspension of Plan Payments

STEP 1: IDENTIFY THE HARDSHIP

Determine the reason you need a temporary suspension. Be specific about how your situation affects your ability to make payments.

STEP 2: GATHER SUPPORTING DOCUMENTS

Collect proof of your hardship, such as pay stubs, bills, or repair invoices. Clear evidence strengthens your request.

STEP 3: PREPARE YOUR REQUEST

Write a formal request to the court, including:

The reason for the suspension

The requested length of time

A statement that you will resume payments after the suspension

STEP 4: FILE THE REQUEST WITH THE COURT

Submit the request and supporting documents to the bankruptcy court and provide copies to the trustee and required parties.

STEP 5: ATTEND THE HEARING (IF REQUIRED)

Explain your hardship clearly and focus on the temporary nature of the suspension. Show the court your commitment to continue the plan once circumstances improve.

STEP 6: RECEIVE COURT DECISION

If approved, payments will be suspended for the specified period. Remember, the plan obligation remains unchanged.

STEP 7: RESUME PAYMENTS AFTER SUSPENSION

Resume payments according to the court's order. If necessary, discuss other modifications or plan adjustments to stay on track.

10 Key Points

1. A bankruptcy moratorium is a legal mechanism that allows you to temporarily postpone your Chapter 13 payment obligations.
2. In Chapter 13 proceedings, a moratorium is a formal legal term with a specific purpose: temporary suspension of plan payments.
3. The process begins by filing a motion—formally known as a Motion to Suspend Plan Payments.
4. Submitting this motion to the bankruptcy court is a required step; it cannot be granted informally or verbally.
5. Only your assigned bankruptcy judge has the authority to approve or deny your suspension request.

6. Valid reasons for suspension include temporary loss of income, unexpected expenses, medical emergencies, or injury/disability.

7. You must show that the hardship is temporary and that you have the ability to recover financially after the suspension.

8. The most common reason debtors request a moratorium is loss of income, often from job loss or reduction of work hours.

9. If approved, most judges grant a suspension lasting about three to six months, depending on your circumstances and evidence.

10. A moratorium provides short-term relief by pausing your payment obligations, giving you a brief and much-needed financial breather.

Chapter 10

Amnesty for Missed Payments

A Chapter 13 debtor who had been making plan payments for two years suddenly faced a major setback when she lost her job, causing her to fall behind on her trustee payments. She understood that missing payments in Chapter 13 could place her entire case at risk of dismissal.

Fortunately, that didn't happen. After she secured new employment, she was able to move forward with her case without being required to immediately make up the payments she had missed.

How did she manage this?

The judge granted her *amnesty* for those delinquent payments.

Amnesty is a special tool in Chapter 13 that **does not reduce your overall plan payments**, but it **does temporarily cut your payment obligations for a limited period**, giving you time to recover from hardship without adding extra pressure.

This legal mechanism has been used by debtors for decades. In this chapter, you'll learn what payment amnesty is, why judges grant it, and how it may protect you if you ever fall behind in your Chapter 13 plan.

Amnesty, Explained

Let's first get this understood—an amnesty is completely different from a payment suspension under Chapter 9. The key distinction is self-explanatory: A suspension delays *future* payments, whereas an amnesty excuses *past*, missed payments. They may seem similar, but they are different in nature.

Dictionary.com defines *amnesty* as either:

- An act of pardoning past transgressions, or
- A deliberate disregard or overlooking of prior offenses.

In bankruptcy, the concept of *amnesty* mirrors the statutory mechanism that allows debtors to be excused for missed plan payments. Although "amnesty" is **not** an official bankruptcy term, we use it in this chapter to highlight a familiar idea: **judicial leniency that excuses past payment obligations without causing your Chapter 13 case to be dismissed**.

A judge cannot grant amnesty on their own. It must be requested by you or your attorney through a plan modification, which operates under the authority of the Bankruptcy Code and allows you to resolve missed payments without having to immediately pay them back.

Defaulting on Plan Payments

During your Chapter 13 case, life can happen—job loss, injury, reduced hours, or unexpected expenses—and these hardships can cause you to fall behind on your plan payments.

When this occurs, both the bankruptcy judge and trustee generally try to work with you. You will usually receive a short grace period to catch up on the missed payments. But if you do not bring the payments current, you will be considered in *default*.

At that point, the trustee issues a *Notice of Material Default*, giving you a set period—often 15 days—to cure the delinquency. If you fail to cure it, your case may face dismissal.

Fortunately, you have options.

One option is to immediately catch up by paying the full amount you owe.

For many debtors, however, this is not realistic. Another option is to request **amnesty** through a plan modification. With a modification request, your arrearages can be thrown into the plan and addressed over time—without any upfront payment. This relief is authorized under the Bankruptcy Code in the provision that permits debtors to cure defaults through modification.

Statutory Provision

This relief stems from **§1322(b)(5)** of the United States Bankruptcy Code, which authorizes a Chapter 13 plan to *cure a default within a reasonable time while maintaining ongoing payments.*

In practical terms, this section allows the court to approve a plan modification that rolls missed payments into the remaining life of the plan, eliminating the need for an immediate lump-sum cure. This is the legal foundation that makes amnesty-style relief possible for debtors who fall behind.

Legal Case Example

In *In re Raymond* (Bankr. S.D. Ohio 1989), debtors Robert and Sue Raymond missed several monthly payments over a four-month period. A creditor responded by filing a motion to dismiss the case.

The judge denied the motion, emphasizing that the debtors had a remedy available. They had the right to seek modification of their plan. That modification would operate as a form of amnesty, allowing them to cure their default and continue under Chapter 13 without dismissal.

Benefits for Curing Material Defaults

The ability to cure missed payments through plan modification offers several major advantages:

1. Avoidance of Dismissal

Debtors can prevent their case from being dismissed even after falling behind.

2. Structured, Manageable Repayment

Missed payments can be handled over time instead of requiring a lump-sum cure.

3. Long-Term Financial Relief

Debtors gain breathing room to stabilize their finances while staying protected under Chapter 13.

What Happens If You Don't Cure the Default?

Failing to cure a material default can place your entire bankruptcy case in jeopardy.

Once you fall behind, you must either bring your plan payments current or request a plan modification to address the missed payments. If you do neither, the consequences are severe:

- **Your Chapter 13 case will be dismissed.**
- **The automatic stay will terminate**, removing the legal shield that protects you from creditors.
- **Creditors can immediately resume collection efforts**, including phone calls, lawsuits, and wage garnishments.
- **Secured creditors may proceed with foreclosure, repossession, or enforcing liens.**
- **You will lose the opportunity to receive a discharge**, meaning none of your dischargeable debts will be forgiven.

Ignoring a payment default can undo all the progress you've made in your Chapter 13 case. Letting the issue linger is never in your best interest.

STEP-BY-STEP GUIDE: Obtaining Amnesty for Missed Plan Payments

STEP 1: IDENTIFY MISSED PLAN PAYMENT(S)

Before taking action, confirm exactly which payments were missed. Missed payments may result from job loss, income reduction, rising expenses, or unexpected emergencies. Regardless of the cause—voluntary or involuntary—the same bankruptcy rules apply: Missed payments must be addressed through a plan modification.

ACTION ITEM:

- Review your trustee payment ledger to verify all missed payments.

STEP 2: CONSULT YOUR ATTORNEY (IF YOU HAVE ONE)

If you are represented, always consult your attorney before filing anything. Bankruptcy lawyers handle modifications regularly and know your judge's preferences.

ACTION ITEM:

- Contact your attorney and inform them of your missed payments and need for modification.

STEP 3: PREPARE THE PLAN MODIFICATION

This involves drafting a motion to modify your Chapter 13 plan, explaining why you missed payments and how you propose to resolve the default. Reasons may include unemployment, medical expenses, reduced income, or other documented hardships.

ACTION ITEM:

- Gather proof of hardship (termination letter, medical bills, etc.).
- Prepare a written explanation for your motion.

STEP 4: FILE THE MOTION WITH YOUR BANKRUPTCY COURT

Submit your motion to the same court where you filed your original bankruptcy case. Under 11 U.S.C. §1322(b)(5), your judge is empowered to approve modifications related to missed payments.

ACTION ITEM:

- File the modification through the court's ECF (electronic filing) system or through your attorney.
- Serve notice to the trustee and all required parties.

STEP 5: WAIT FOR COURT APPROVAL / HEARING (IF REQUIRED)

The court may approve your modification automatically or schedule a hearing depending on your district.

Once approved, your missed payments are **added to the remaining plan months**, meaning:

- **You owe nothing immediately**
- **Your default is cured**
- **Your case remains active**

Even if your attorney charges fees, those fees may also be included in your plan—requiring ***no upfront payment***.

ACTION ITEM:

- Check your docket periodically to confirm approval.

10 Key Points

1. You may request amnesty if you miss plan payments.
2. Only your bankruptcy judge can grant this amnesty.
3. Amnesty is obtained through a plan modification.
4. Missed payments may result from voluntary or involuntary causes.
5. A *Notice of Material Default* will be issued after missed payments.
6. The Notice gives about 15 days to cure the default.
7. You cure the default by paying the arrears or filing a motion to modify.
8. Your motion must be filed with your bankruptcy court.
9. A hearing may be held depending on your judge.
10. Once approved, the missed payments are included in your plan, with no lump-sum required.

Chapter 11

No Proof to Your Claim

When you file for Chapter 13 bankruptcy, creditors don't get to sit back as if they're relaxing on a beach in Hawaii. They have a job to do—and the clock starts ticking immediately. One of their most important responsibilities is filing a **Proof of Claim (POC)**. (Throughout this chapter, we'll often refer to it simply as a "claim.")

Here's where things get interesting:

If a creditor fails to file a claim, that failure can work **in your favor**. A missing, late, or defective claim may create an opportunity to *lower* your Chapter 13 plan payments.

Fasten your seat belt—this chapter reveals a little-known strategy that many debtors never learn. By the end, you'll understand:

1. **How the claim system works,** and
2. **How a creditor's failure to file—or file incorrectly—can reduce your plan payments.**

What Is a Claim?

A claim, short for Proof of Claim (POC), is the document a creditor must file if they want to be paid in your Chapter 13 case. It tells the bankruptcy court:

- "I'm owed money,"
- "Here's how much," and
- "Here's the paperwork proving it."

If the creditor does **not** file a claim, they do not have an enforceable claim in the case and generally receive *no payment*.

A proper claim must:

- State the amount owed as of the bankruptcy filing date
- Include supporting documents (contracts, agreements, statements, payment histories)
- Comply with Federal Rule of Bankruptcy Procedure 3001(c)(1), which requires the writing on which the claim is based or an explanation if the writing is unavailable

This ensures accuracy and prevents inflated, false, or incomplete claims.

Sidebar about the Claim

- A claim is a creditor's ticket into your plan.
- No claim = no payment.
- Documentation is mandatory—not optional.
- Every claim must be filed before the **bar date** (the deadline).

Why the Claim Matters?

The claim is the backbone of the claim registry process because it accomplishes three primary tasks:

1. Notice of the Debt

It formally notifies the court, trustee, and other creditors that a specific debt exists and payment is being requested.

2. Establishing the Amount Owed

It sets the exact amount the creditor asserts—including principal, interest, and fees. The trustee uses this amount to determine how much creditors receive.

3. Verification

Supporting documents allow your attorney to:

- confirm accuracy
- detect illegal or inflated fees
- identify miscalculated balances
- challenge improper or defective claims

If the paperwork is incomplete, inaccurate, or missing, the claim can be **objected to** and **disallowed**.

ILLUSTRATION: HOW A CLAIM IS "BORN" IN BANKRUPTCY

Creditor (has debt)
↓
Creditor completes claim form
↓
Creditor attaches required documents
↓
Creditor files claim before bar date
↓
Trustee reviews → claim becomes part of your plan

Time to File the Claim: Deadlines

The bar date is critical. Missing it usually means the creditor does not get paid.

Non-Governmental Creditors:

Must file within 70 days of the petition date.

Governmental Creditors:

Have 180 days from the petition date to file.

When a creditor fails to file a claim, the claim is disallowed and no payment is issued—the same results occur when a claim is filed but is *defective*. Either situation can directly benefit you because invalid or unfiled claims are excluded from repayment, potentially lowering your Chapter 13 plan payments.

No claim. No payment.

The Claim: Using It as a Tool to Cut Your Plan Payments

Even if your plan is already confirmed, the **Trustee's Recommendation Concerning Claims (TRCC)** stage allows adjustments based on which claims were filed properly.

The TRCC Stage

The TRCC occurs after the deadline (claims bar date) for creditors to file their claim. At this stage, the trustee reviews:

- which creditors filed valid claims
- which filed late
- which filed defective or incomplete claims
- which failed to file at all

Each claim is classified as:

✓ **Allowed, or**

✗ **Disallowed**

If there's a deficiency in the claim form, that debt is eliminated from your plan. Your total repayment amount drops immediately. Texas bankruptcy attorney Chance M. McGhee calls this effect "dollar-for-dollar debt reduction." See the below illustration.

Sample Illustration

Original Unsecured Debt: $30,000
Creditor A (filed): $10,000
Creditor B (filed): $15,000
Creditor C (**improper claim**): $5,000

New Total Unsecured Debt: $25,000
Result: Monthly plan payment decreases.

Case in Point: Marcus's Plan Reduction

Marcus's confirmed plan required $500 per month for 60 months to repay $30,000 in unsecured debt. During the TRCC stage, his attorney discovered a creditor with a $5,000 claim failed to file a claim.

The claim was ***disallowed***, reducing his unsecured debt to $25,000. Marcus's attorney filed a modification, and his payment dropped from $500 to about $417.

A **small** creditor mistake produced a **big** impact.

STEP-BY-STEP GUIDE: Reducing Plan Payments During the TRCC

Step One: Obtain the TRCC Notice / Creditor Registry

- Request a copy from your trustee or attorney.
- It lists all creditors and claim amounts.
- It shows which creditors filed a claim and which did not.

Step Two: Review the TRCC Notice / Creditor Registry

Look for unsecured creditors who:

- did **not** file a claim
- filed a **late** claim
- submitted **inaccurate** claim information
- failed to attach required documentation

Any of these defects can lead to a claim being **disallowed**, reducing your repayment amount.

SIDEBAR: STEP TWO INSIGHT

Not all disallowed claims result from missing claims.

- Late filings
- Incorrect amounts
- Missing documents
- Errors or inconsistencies
- Wrong creditor filing the claim

All can lead to **disallowance**.

Each disallowed claim = **less debt to include in the plan**, giving you a chance to lower payments.

Step Three: Take Detailed Notes

Document:

- each creditor with a missing, late, or defective claim
- the amount claimed
- the defect you identified

These notes help your attorney file objections or motions.

Step Four: Contact Your Attorney

Provide your notes and findings. Your attorney will verify the issues and challenge improper claims.

Step Five: Request a Plan Modification

Once defective or missing claims are disallowed, request a modification of your confirmed plan.

Disallowed claims reduce your total unsecured debt →
Your plan payments can be *reduced proportionally.*

10 Key Points

1. When you file Chapter 13, the court notifies all creditors.
2. Unsecured creditors must file a Proof of Claim (POC) to be paid.
3. The claim is the creditor's formal request for payment.
4. Non-governmental creditors must file within 70 days (not 90).
5. Many creditors fail to file timely or proper claims.
6. The TRCC occurs after the bar date.
7. Claims are labeled allowed or disallowed at TRCC.
8. Missing or defective claims can benefit you.
9. Without a proper claim, the creditor receives no repayment.
10. You may request a plan modification to reduce payments based on disallowed debt.

Chapter 12

Increased Living Expenses: How Legitimate Expenses Can Lower Your Monthly Payments

One often-overlooked strategy to reduce Chapter 13 plan payments is documenting increased necessary expenses.

These are costs that the court recognizes as essential for maintaining your household. When these expenses rise—or reach the IRS or court-allowed maximum—your **disposable income decreases**, providing a legitimate basis to **seek a lower monthly plan payment** through a §1329 modification.

Necessary Expenses, Explained

Necessary expenses are the costs that are considered essential to maintain a debtor's household and basic standard of living. The court evaluates these expenses when determining ***disposable income***, which directly affects your Chapter 13 plan payment.

Typical categories of necessary expenses include:

- **Housing:** Rent or mortgage, property taxes, homeowners/renters insurance
- **Utilities:** Electricity, water, gas, trash, internet, phone
- **Food & Household Supplies:** Groceries, cleaning supplies, basic household items
- **Transportation:** Car payments, fuel, insurance, routine maintenance

- **Healthcare:** Insurance premiums, medications, essential medical treatment
- **Childcare or Elder Care:** Payments for dependents or elderly family members

Key Point:

Expenses must be reasonable and documented. The court may allow adjustments if expenses increase or reach the IRS/court-allowed maximum.

How Increased Expenses Affect Plan Payments

Chapter 13 plan payments are calculated using the disposable income formula:

Disposable Income = Income – Necessary Expenses

When necessary expenses increase—or rise to the allowable maximum— disposable income decreases. This reduction can legally lower your plan payment. Courts recognize this and allow debtors to adjust payments when these expenses increase, even mid-plan.

Board-Certified Attorney Vicky Fealy addressed this in her blog post, *When Inflation Makes Your Texas Chapter 13 Unworkable*. She explained that our current economy makes some debtors' plans no longer feasible. She further noted that debtors can file a §1329 modification to adjust their plan payments when necessary expenses unexpectedly rise.

Types of Expense Increases That Can Reduce Plan Payments

1. Necessary Household Expenses

These include everyday costs required for basic living as listed earlier.

2. 401(k) Loan Changes

401(k) loans affect take-home pay and disposable income:

- **New loan repayments** reduce disposable income
- **Loan termination or payoff** can free up cash to cover necessary expenses, indirectly reducing plan payments if adjustments are requested

3. New Priority Debts

Certain newly arising priority debts can affect the calculation of disposable income:

- Court-ordered taxes or government claims
- Wage claims or other legally prioritized debts

4. New Secured Debt

Debtors may need to take on new secured debt for essential purposes, such as purchasing another vehicle, acquiring necessary equipment, or making critical home improvements.

- **Court Approval Required:**
  Any new secured debt must be requested from the bankruptcy court. The debtor files a motion explaining the need for the purchase, how it is essential, and how it will be repaid.
- **Effect on Plan Payments:**
  Once approved, the monthly payment for the new secured debt is added as an allowed expense, which can reduce disposable income and therefore lower your Chapter 13 plan payment.

The common thread, *across all scenarios*, is that any documented increase in necessary household expenses, or any expense that reaches the IRS or court-allowed maximum, reduces disposable income. This provides a legal and recognized reason to request a lower plan payment through a §1329 modification.

Step-by-Step Guide: Using Increased Living Expenses to Lower Chapter 13 Plan Payments

Step 1: Identify Your Necessary Living Expenses

Begin by listing all household expenses that are considered *necessary* under bankruptcy standards. These are expenses required to maintain a basic standard of living, not discretionary or luxury items.

Step 2: Compare Your Expenses to IRS and Court Guidelines

Review IRS National and Local Standards and any applicable court guidelines. If your actual expenses are below these allowable amounts, increases up to the maximum may still be considered reasonable and permissible.

Step 3: Track Any Increases Carefully

Document when and how your necessary expenses increase. Common triggers include inflation, rent increases, higher utility bills, rising insurance premiums, medical needs, or transportation costs.

Step 4: Gather Supporting Documentation

Collect proof of increased expenses, such as:

- Updated leases or mortgage statements
- Utility bills
- Insurance premium notices
- Medical bills or prescriptions
- Childcare or elder-care invoices

Courts rely heavily on documentation.

Step 5: Recalculate Disposable Income

Apply the Chapter 13 formula:

Disposable Income = Income − Necessary Expenses

As necessary expenses rise, disposable income decreases.

Step 6: Determine Plan Feasibility

Assess whether your current plan payment is still realistic given your updated expense profile. If expenses now consume more of your income, your plan may no longer be feasible as confirmed.

Step 7: Consult with Counsel About §1329

A §1329 modification is the legal mechanism to adjust payments after confirmation. Discuss whether your expense increases justify a modification request.

Step 8: File a §1329 Modification Motion

The modification request should clearly explain:

- Which expenses increased
- Why the increases are necessary
- How they reduce disposable income

Step 9: Address Any Objections

Trustees or creditors may question reasonableness. Proper documentation and alignment with IRS or court standards strengthen your position.

Step 10: Obtain Court Approval and Adjust Payments

Once approved, your revised plan payment becomes effective, reflecting your updated financial reality.

10 Key Points

1. Necessary expenses directly reduce disposable income, which is the foundation of Chapter 13 plan payments.

2. Courts recognize inflation and cost-of-living increases as legitimate reasons to revisit plan feasibility.

3. Expenses must be reasonable, necessary, and documented—unsupported claims are unlikely to succeed.

4. IRS and court-allowed maximums matter; reaching or approaching them strengthens modification requests.

5. Housing, utilities, food, transportation, healthcare, and dependent care are core expense categories reviewed by trustees.

6. 401(k) loan changes affect take-home pay, which can indirectly alter disposable income calculations.

7. New priority debts, such as taxes or government claims, may lawfully reduce funds available for plan payments.

8. New secured debt requires court approval, but once approved, the payment becomes an allowable expense.

9. Mid-plan changes are permitted under §1329, even if the original plan was feasible when confirmed.

10. The common thread is necessity—any legitimate increase in required living expenses provides a recognized legal basis to lower Chapter 13 plan payments.

Chapter 13
Ending Your Chapter 13 Payments Through a Conversion

In Chapter 13 bankruptcy, you're required to make monthly trustee payments for three to five years. But what if there were a legitimate way to end those payments much sooner?

There is—and it's one of the most foolproof ways to eliminate your plan payments.

By converting your case to Chapter 7, you can stop making plan payments far earlier than you would under a full Chapter 13 repayment period—while still receiving a successful discharge. In this chapter, you'll learn exactly how a Chapter 7 conversion works and how it can provide a faster, more direct path to resolving your debt.

Before diving into the mechanics of the conversion process, let's begin by understanding the key differences between Chapter 13 and Chapter 7.

DIFFERENCE BETWEEN CHAPTER 13 AND CHAPTER 7

Most personal bankruptcies in the United States are filed under Chapter 13 or Chapter 7. Although both are designed for individuals, they operate very differently. Understanding these differences will help you see why converting from Chapter 13 to Chapter 7 can immediately dispose your monthly plan payments.

Chapter 13 Bankruptcy

Chapter 13—often called *reorganization bankruptcy*—requires you to repay some or all of your debts over a 3–5 year period.

Key Features

- 3–5 year repayment plan. You pay the trustee every month.
- Regular income required.
- You keep your assets as long as the plan pays creditors what they would have received in a Chapter 7 liquidation.
- Can catch up on secured debt, such as mortgages, car loans, or tax arrears.

Advantages

- Protects property from repossession or foreclosure.
- Allows structured repayment of overdue secured debts.
- Provides a path to discharge remaining unsecured debts after plan completion.

Disadvantages

- Requires strict budgeting for years.
- Long, complex process.

Higher financial stress if income drops.

Chapter 7 Bankruptcy

Chapter 7—often called *straight bankruptcy*—is the faster and simpler option. It wipes out most unsecured debt and typically lasts only a few months.

Key Features

- **Eliminates unsecured debt.** Credit cards, medical bills, payday loans, and old utility debts are usually discharged.
- **Qualification is based on income.** Most people qualify through the *means test*, which compares your income to your state's median income.
- **Little to no repayment.** You do not make ongoing payments to a trustee.

The Means Test (Simplified)

1. **Compare your income to your state's median income.**
   If you are at or below the median, you qualify automatically.
2. **If you are above the median, a second calculation is required.**
   The court subtracts allowed expenses (housing, food, transportation, insurance, etc.) from your income.
   If there is not enough remaining disposable income to repay creditors, you qualify for Chapter 7.

What Chapter 7 Offers?

- A quick discharge (usually in 2–3 months).
- No repayment plan.
- A fresh start if you qualify under the means test.

CONVERSION FROM CHAPTER 13 TO CHAPTER 7

If your Chapter 13 plan becomes unaffordable—or you simply no longer need the repayment plan—converting your case to Chapter 7 can be the fastest and most effective way to do away with your monthly trustee payments.

As Nolo notes, conversion is often an excellent option when a debtor cannot maintain payments and does not qualify for a plan modification.

Your Legal Right to Convert

Under 11 U.S.C. § 1307, you have the right to convert your Chapter 13 case to a Chapter 7 case at any time.

There is **no waiting period** and no limitation on when you may request the conversion.

Think of it like throwing in the towel in a boxing match: you can stop the fight—and your plan payments—whenever you choose.

The One Major Exception

If you received a **Chapter 7 discharge within the last 8 years**, you *cannot* convert your Chapter 13 case into a Chapter 7 case.

Example:

A debtor filed Chapter 13 to save a vehicle. He had already received a Chapter 7 discharge six years earlier. After deciding to surrender the vehicle, he asked to convert to Chapter 7.

The court denied the conversion because federal law barred him from receiving another Chapter 7 discharge so soon.

If you have **not** filed Chapter 7 in the last 8 years, this restriction does not apply.

THE MEANS TEST AFTER CONVERSION

A common question arises:

Do you have to take the means test when converting from Chapter 13 to Chapter 7?

Courts disagree:

Some courts say NO.

They hold that the right to convert is absolute and cannot be restricted by the means test.

Other courts say YES.

They believe all Chapter 7 cases—whether filed directly or reached through conversion—require the means test.

Because this issue varies by location, your bankruptcy attorney is the best source of guidance. They will know how your specific district handles the means test after a conversion.

THE BOTTOM LINE

Switching from Chapter 13 to Chapter 7 is a powerful option.
It can:

- ***Instantly eliminate your monthly plan payments***, and
- Provide a ***fresh financial start*** much sooner than completing a 3–5 year repayment plan.

CONVERSION IS THE KEY TO ENDING YOUR MONTHLY TRUSTEE PAYMENTS FOR GOOD

For many Chapter 13 debtors, the biggest burden isn't the debt itself—it's the long-term commitment to making monthly trustee payments for three to five years. When income drops, expenses rise, or life simply becomes unpredictable, those payments can feel impossible to maintain.

This is where conversion becomes the key.

Once you convert your Chapter 13 case to Chapter 7, your obligation to make monthly trustee payments stops **immediately**. There is no waiting period, no approval process, and no requirement to finish the remaining months of your plan. The conversion officially closes the door on the Chapter 13 repayment structure and replaces it with a faster, simpler Chapter 7 process.

For debtors who qualify, conversion isn't just an option—**it's the most powerful tool to end plan payments permanently.**

Consider the case of a debtor who entered Chapter 13 to save his vehicle and reorganize his debt. At first, the monthly trustee payments seemed manageable. But over time, unexpected events hit hard:

- his work hours were cut,
- his vehicle needed repairs,
- and the rising cost of living drained every spare dollar.

His plan payment—once tolerable—became overwhelming. Each month he found himself choosing between groceries, gas, and the trustee payment. The stress mounted, and he fell behind.

Instead of allowing the case to fail, he chose to convert to Chapter 7.

Within weeks of filing the conversion notice:

- **All plan payments stopped,**
- **His unsecured debts were wiped out,**
- and **the financial pressure that had been crushing him disappeared almost overnight.**

By the time his Chapter 7 discharge was entered, he described the result in one sentence:

"It felt like someone finally lifted the weight off my chest."

His experience reflects what thousands of debtors discover each year: ***Conversion can instantly end your plan payments and give you the instant fresh start Chapter 13 could not deliver.***

WHAT HAPPENS AFTER A CHAPTER 7 CONVERSION?

Converting your Chapter 13 case to Chapter 7 comes with new responsibilities. To ensure a smooth transition and compliance with bankruptcy rules, here's what you need to know:

1. Attend a New 341 Meeting

After the conversion, a new **meeting of creditors** (also called the 341 hearing) will be scheduled.
At this hearing, creditors may ask questions about your financial situation and the reasons for the conversion.

2. Update Schedules I and J

You must update **Schedules I and J,** which detail your income and expenses. These updates ensure the court has an accurate picture of your current financial situation.

3. Reassess Exemptions

Exemptions protect certain assets from being used to pay creditors. After conversion, you may need to **reassess or update your claimed exemptions,** as rules can differ between Chapter 13 and Chapter 7.

4. Work with a New Trustee

A new **trustee** will be appointed. The trustee's role includes:

- Reviewing your case
- Ensuring compliance with bankruptcy laws
- Managing liquidation of non-exempt assets

HOW LONG DOES IT TAKE TO RECEIVE A CHAPTER 7 DISCHARGE?

Typically, it takes 2 to 3 months from the conversion date to receive your discharge.

REQUIRED COURSES AFTER CHAPTER 7 CONVERSION

All Chapter 7 debtors must complete a **financial management course** (debtor education course) before receiving a discharge.

Key Points:

1. **Timing:** Must be completed after filing your Chapter 7 petition and before your discharge.
2. **Approved Providers:** The course must be taken from a provider approved by the **U.S. Trustee Program**. A list of approved providers is available on the U.S. Trustee's website or through the bankruptcy court.
3. **Content:** Covers budgeting, managing money, using credit wisely, and preparing for financial stability post-bankruptcy.
4. **Proof of Completion:** You will receive a certificate, which must be filed with the court. Failure to file the certificate can result in dismissal of your case without a discharge.
5. **Consequences of Non-Compliance:** Not completing the course or filing the certificate means your debts will not be discharged, and creditors can resume collection.
6. **Cost:** While there is a fee, providers are required to reduce or waive it if you cannot afford it.

Completing this course is **essential**. It is one of the final steps to successfully completing your Chapter 7 bankruptcy.

RETAINING SECURED PROPERTY IN CHAPTER 7

If you want to keep a secured asset (like a car or home), you must file a **Statement of Intention**, which tells the court and creditors what you plan to do with your secured property.

You have three options:

1. **Surrender the Property**

   o   Give the property back to the lender.
   o   Any remaining debt is discharged.
   o   This is the simplest option.

2. **Reaffirm the Debt**

   o   Sign a **Reaffirmation Agreement** with the creditor.
   o   You agree to continue paying the debt under the same or new terms.
   o   This allows you to keep the property.

3. **Redeem the Property**

   o   Pay the creditor the current value of the property in a lump sum.
   o   After redemption, you retain the property free of any other debt.

STEP-BY-STEP GUIDE: Converting Your Chapter 13 Case to Chapter

Many debtors consider converting their Chapter 13 case to Chapter 7 primarily to **eliminate monthly plan payments**. If you're one of them, the process is straightforward. Follow these steps to make the conversion as smooth as possible.

STEP 1: Evaluate Secured Property and Nonpriority Debt

Before converting, review your debts carefully:

- **Payment Status:** Are your secured and nonpriority unsecured debts already paid in full? If yes, conversion is an option.

- **Property Retention:** Do you want to keep secured property (like a car or home) protected under Chapter 13?

  o If not, surrendering the property allows a faster Chapter 7 process, usually completed within a few months.

- **Settlement Possibilities:** Can you negotiate directly with creditors outside bankruptcy?

  o If yes, a **Reaffirmation Agreement** may be required when converting to Chapter 7.

STEP 2: Consult Your Attorney

Contact your bankruptcy attorney before taking any steps. Your attorney will:

- Explain the implications of converting,
- Guide you on legal requirements, and
- Ensure all filings are accurate and timely.

STEP 3: Assess the Means Test Requirement

Determine whether you must pass the Chapter 7 means test.

- Some jurisdictions require the means test even for conversions; others do not.
- Your attorney will know your court's rules and confirm whether it applies to your case.

STEP 4: File a Notice of Conversion / Motion to Convert

Submit a Notice of Conversion (or Motion to Convert) to the bankruptcy court.

- This informs the court and your creditors of your intention to switch from Chapter 13 to Chapter 7.
- No hearing is required in most cases.

STEP 5: Transition and Finalize the Case

Once your case is converted:

- A **Chapter 7 trustee** is appointed to review your case, oversee any liquidation of non-exempt assets, and ensure compliance.
- Your **monthly Chapter 13 payments stop immediately**.
- You complete the Chapter 7 requirements, including updating Schedules I and J and taking the **debtor education course**.
- The trustee notifies your employer to stop wage garnishments (if applicable).

STEP 6: Receive Your Chapter 7 Discharge

- Within a few months, you should receive a bankruptcy discharge, wiping out eligible unsecured debts.
- Your obligation to make Chapter 13 plan payments ends permanently, giving you a fresh financial start.

Pro Tip: Conversion is often the most reliable way to end monthly trustee payments, especially if your Chapter 13 plan has become unmanageable. Talk to your attorney early to make the process seamless.

10 Key Points

1. You have a legal right to convert your Chapter 13 case to Chapter 7.

2. This right is absolute and cannot be denied by the court.

3. You can convert at any time during your Chapter 13 case.

4. If you received a Chapter 7 discharge within the last 8 years, you cannot convert your Chapter 13 case.

5. Chapter 7 and Chapter 13 operate very differently—conversion changes the structure of your bankruptcy and your obligations.

6. Converting to Chapter 7 imposes new responsibilities, including attending a new 341 meeting, working with a Chapter 7 trustee, and updating financial schedules.

7. In some jurisdictions, the conversion may require you to pass the Chapter 7 means test.

8. You may choose to reaffirm secured debts (e.g., a vehicle) through a Reaffirmation Agreement if you want to retain the property.

9. After conversion, a Chapter 7 discharge is typically granted within approximately 2–3 months.

10. A primary reason for converting is to eliminate monthly Chapter 13 plan payments and relieve financial burden.

Chapter 14
Hardship Discharge

There's a classic line by Run-DMC that goes: *"Hard times spreading just like the flu. Watch out, homeboy, don't let it catch you."* In bankruptcy, those words couldn't be more true. When hard times catch up to you—unexpected job loss, medical bills, or other financial setbacks—you still have options.

Most people assume their choices are limited: convert to Chapter 7, suspend plan payments, or dismiss the case entirely. But for many debtors, these solutions simply aren't enough.

That's where the hardship discharge comes in—a little-known lifeline written into the Bankruptcy Code. If you qualify, a hardship discharge can eliminate the rest of your plan payments and give you a fresh start when it feels like all hope is lost.

What Is a Hardship Discharge?

When you filed Chapter 13, you created a reorganization plan. This plan placed you on a strict budget and required you to repay creditors through monthly trustee payments.

But sometimes, life takes a turn—medical emergencies, job loss, disability, or other events beyond your control may make it impossible to continue. In these situations, the Bankruptcy Code allows you to request a hardship discharge.

A hardship discharge ends your plan early and grants a discharge even though you did not complete all required payments.

Requirements for a Hardship Discharge

Under 11 U.S.C. § 1328(b), you must satisfy ***all three*** of the following:

1. **Circumstances Beyond Your Control** — Something happened that prevents you from making plan payments, and it is not your fault.
2. **Creditors Paid Equitably** — Unsecured creditors have already received at least what they would have received in a Chapter 7 liquidation.
3. **Plan Modification Is Not Practical** — Your plan cannot be modified to reduce payments further.

You must file a motion and provide evidence supporting each requirement.

First Requirement: Inability to Complete Payments

You must show that circumstances outside your control prevent you from continuing with the plan.

How Courts Used to View This Requirement

Courts once applied a very strict "catastrophic circumstances" test. Temporary job loss or short-term disability was not enough; total disability or permanent inability to work was usually required.

The Modern Standard

Today, courts apply the more flexible **"unforeseen economic circumstances"** test. Sudden job loss or unexpected financial collapse may qualify even if the condition isn't permanent.

For example, in the case involving **Cinda Suzanne Dior**, the court granted a hardship discharge after she unexpectedly lost her job and could not secure new employment despite good-faith efforts.

Common Circumstances That May Qualify

- Physical or mental illness
- Serious injury
- Total disability
- Death of the debtor
- Death of a close family member
- Loss of income
- Divorce or separation

You must show how the event directly prevents continued funding of the plan, even with a modification. Evidence is essential.

Second Requirement: Creditors Must Be Adequately Compensated

Unsecured creditors must have received at least as much as they would in a Chapter 7 case.

How This Is Measured

This depends on your **nonexempt property**—the assets that would be available to sell in a Chapter 7 liquidation:

- Cash or bank balances
- Stocks and bonds
- A second home
- A second vehicle
- Valuable collections
- Expensive instruments or equipment

If You Have No Nonexempt Property

You have a "no-asset" case; creditors would receive nothing in Chapter 7. Therefore, this requirement is automatically met.

If You Do Have Nonexempt Property

You must show that unsecured creditors have already been paid an amount equal to—or greater than—the value of that property.

Third Requirement: Plan Modification Is Not Practical

You must show that reducing your plan payments further is not possible.

Your attorney typically files a motion to modify the plan when income drops. But if you are already paying the lowest amount the law allows—or no workable modification exists—you satisfy this requirement. As attorney Kitty J. Lin notes, once a debtor reaches the legal minimum, further reductions are impossible.

Example Using a Fictionalized Cartoon Character

To understand how a hardship discharge works, imagine a well-known cartoon character—let's call him **"Mickey Mouse"**—in a Chapter 13 case.

At first, Mickey's animation studio is thriving, and he makes payments without issue. Halfway through the plan, the studio suddenly closes after losing its biggest production contract. Overnight, Mickey's income collapses, and he can no longer afford the plan payments.

His attorney explores modification but discovers Mickey is already paying the legal minimum. No further reductions are allowed. With income gone and modification unavailable, a hardship discharge becomes the only viable option.

Requirement 1: Circumstances Beyond His Control

The studio shutdown was sudden, unexpected, and outside Mickey's control. This satisfies the first requirement.

Requirement 2: Creditors Paid Adequately

Mickey owns little or no nonexempt property. In a hypothetical Chapter 7, unsecured creditors would receive nothing. Since they have already received more than zero in his Chapter 13, the second requirement is satisfied.

Requirement 3: Modification Is Not Practical

Mickey is already paying the legal minimum, so modification is impossible. The third requirement is met.

All three elements line up. Mickey qualifies for a hardship discharge.

STEP-BY-STEP GUIDE: Using a Hardship Discharge to Eliminate Plan Payments

STEP 1 — Talk with Your Attorney

Notify your attorney immediately about the event that affected your income. Your attorney will evaluate your eligibility under §1328(b) and advise on next steps.

STEP 2 — Gather Evidence

Collect documents proving the hardship and showing your financial condition, such as:

- Medical records or disability statements
- Termination letters or unemployment notices
- SSI/SSDI termination or award letters
- Pay stubs, P&L statements, tax returns
- Job-search documentation
- Death notices and estate documents
- Proof of exemptions and nonexempt property

- Trustee payment history
- A sworn affidavit describing the hardship

Organize these into a coherent evidence packet.

STEP 3 — Prepare the Motion

Your attorney drafts the motion and supporting declarations, including:

- The event causing the hardship
- Evidence supporting the Chapter 7 comparison
- Proof that modification isn't workable
- A proposed order
- A certificate of service

STEP 4 — File and Serve the Motion

Your attorney files the motion and serves:
- The Chapter 13 trustee
- All relevant creditors

STEP 5 — Expect Objections

Prepare for objections regarding:

- Whether the hardship was unforeseeable
- The valuation of nonexempt assets
- Whether modification was possible

STEP 6 — Attend the Hearing

The judge reviews evidence and decides whether all three statutory requirements have been met. You may need to testify briefly.

STEP 7 — Court Decision

The judge will either:

- **Grant** the hardship discharge, ending plan payments and discharging eligible debts, or
- **Deny** the motion, in which case you and your attorney can consider alternatives (appeal, renewed motion, modification, conversion, or dismissal).

10 Key Points

1. Unexpected hardship after filing Chapter 13 is common.
2. A hardship discharge applies when an unforeseen event prevents plan funding.
3. You may request one if you have good cause.
4. You must meet all three requirements under 11 U.S.C. § 1328(b).
5. Strong evidence is essential.
6. Some districts provide a hardship-discharge motion template online.
7. The motion is filed in the same court where your case was opened.
8. The court will schedule a hearing.
9. Common qualifying hardships include illness, disability, and loss of income.
10. A hardship discharge lets you complete bankruptcy earlier than scheduled.

Chapter 15

The Cramdown Game: Winning on Your Car Loan in Chapter 13

Filing for Chapter 13 bankruptcy can feel like stepping into a high-stakes game, and one of the most important pieces on the board is your vehicle. A car isn't just a luxury—it's how you get to work, run errands, and keep daily life moving.

But if your vehicle isn't fully paid off, it can also be a major source of stress. That's where the Chapter 13 "cramdown" comes in—a legal move that can significantly reduce your car loan payments and lower your overall Chapter 13 plan payment.

Before you start strategizing, you need to *remember* one simple number:

910

Counting the Days

The first step is to calculate how long it's been since you bought your car. Why? Because timing is everything in the cramdown game. If your vehicle loan was taken out **more than 910 days** before you filed for bankruptcy—roughly 2.5 years—you may qualify to "cram down" the loan to the car's current market value. That means you don't have to pay the full original loan amount—just what the car is worth today.

If your purchase was **within the 910-day window**, you're stuck paying the full loan amount as part of your Chapter 13 plan. That's the rule, and there's no wiggle room. But if you're outside that window, your car loan can be reduced, giving you a clear path to lower your Chapter 13 plan payment and free up money for other debts or living expenses.

The Law Behind the Lucky Number

The 910-day rule comes from the **Bankruptcy Abuse Prevention and Consumer Protection Act of 2005 (BAPCPA)** and is applied through **11 U.S.C. § 1325(a)**—specifically the "hanging paragraph" following §1325(a)(9). In simple terms, it protects lenders from borrowers who purchase a car shortly before filing bankruptcy.

But if you bought your vehicle long enough ago, the law allows you to adjust the loan to match your car's present market value, giving you a legal pathway to reduce your secured debt and your monthly plan payment.

Example:
Larry owes $15,000 on his car, but it's only worth $10,000 today.
Under a cramdown:

- The **secured portion** becomes $10,000.
- The remaining **$5,000 becomes unsecured debt**.

Unsecured debts often receive very little—or sometimes nothing—in a Chapter 13 plan. Bonus: the interest rate on the secured portion is usually reduced too.

Enter the Cramdown

The term "cramdown" might sound intense, and that's fitting. It means modifying a loan **against the lender's original terms**. If your vehicle qualifies under the 910-day rule, the lender can object, but they **cannot stop the cramdown**.

You reduce the secured portion of the loan to the car's market value. Any remaining balance becomes unsecured.

In short, the cramdown gives you *leverage* and a legal way to reduce a major expense, lower your Chapter 13 plan payments, and keep your vehicle without overpaying.

Example: How a Cramdown Lowers Your Chapter 13 Plan Payments

Meet Sandra (a fictional example)

Sandra bought her car 1,150 days before she filed for Chapter 13—well past the 910-day threshold. She still owes $18,500 on the car loan, but the vehicle's current market value has dropped to $11,200. Under normal (non-bankruptcy) terms, she's stuck paying the full $18,500 plus her original high interest rate. But because she qualifies for a cramdown, here's what happens:

Step 1: Reduce the Secured Portion

- Original loan balance: $18,500
- Current value: $11,200
- **Secured amount becomes: $11,200**

Step 2: Reclassify the Rest

- Remaining **$7,300** becomes unsecured debt.

Step 3: Lower the Interest Rate

- Original interest: **13.9%**
- Chapter 13 interest: **6%**

Step 4: Payment Drops

- Before: $476/month
- After cramdown: $247/month
- Savings: $229/month

Step 5: Impact on Her Chapter 13 Plan

Because secured payments drive plan calculations:

- Lower secured debt →
- Lower plan base →
- Lower monthly plan payment.

Her total plan payment drops from **$915** to **$670** per month.

A **$245/month** reduction—just from the cramdown.

STEP-BY-STEP GUIDE: Using the Cramdown to Lower Chapter 13 Payments

STEP 1 — VERIFY ELIGIBILITY FOR THE 910 RULE

What to do: Confirm the vehicle was purchased more than 910 days before filing.

Why it matters: This threshold determines whether the loan can be reduced to the car's current value.

Tip: Count days precisely. If the loan was incurred within 910 days, a cramdown is unavailable for a purchase-money car loan.

STEP 2 — CONSULT WITH YOUR ATTORNEY

What to do: Discuss eligibility and strategy.

Why it matters: Your attorney will confirm the 910-day calculation, evaluate exceptions (e.g., business-use vehicles, non-purchase-money liens), and prepare the modification.

Tip: Bring loan documents, purchase contract, and your filing date.

STEP 3 — FILE A MOTION TO MODIFY YOUR PLAN

What to do: Your attorney files a motion requesting the cramdown.

Why it matters: This officially notifies the court and the lender.

Tip: Ensure the motion specifies the vehicle, loan amount, and cramdown basis.

STEP 4 — GATHER EVIDENCE OF MARKET VALUE

What to do: Obtain reliable valuation evidence (appraisal, NADA/KBB printout, dealer offer).

Why it matters: The court needs objective proof of the car's value.

Tip: Use recent, dated valuations.

STEP 5 — PREPARE SUPPORTING DOCUMENTATION

What to do: Collect loan statements, purchase contracts, title information, and appraisal.

Why it matters: These documents support the cramdown facts.

Tip: Include proof of the lender's lien.

STEP 6 — ATTEND THE MODIFICATION HEARING

What to do: Appear (or your attorney appears) and present evidence.

Why it matters: The court reviews the valuation and hears objections.

Tip: Expect objections and be prepared to explain eligibility.

STEP 7 — COURT REVIEW AND DECISION

What to do: The court approves, modifies, or denies the cramdown.
Why it matters: Approval reduces the secured portion and modifies the plan.
Tip: If denied, ask about appeal or alternative plan options.

STEP 8 — RECLASSIFY THE REMAINING BALANCE

What to do: Any amount above market value becomes unsecured.
Why it matters: Unsecured debt usually receives a lower payout.
Tip: Review your plan's unsecured distribution terms.

STEP 9 — REQUEST A LOWER INTEREST RATE

What to do: Ask the court to set a reasonable cramdown interest rate.
Why it matters: A lower rate means lower payments.
Tip: Courts often use the *prime + risk adjustment* formula.

STEP 10 — IMPLEMENT THE MODIFIED PLAN

What to do: Once approved, the modified plan becomes binding.
Why it matters: These are your new payment obligations.
Tip: Confirm the trustee and creditor update their records.

10 Key Points

1. A vehicle loan must be older than 910 days before the bankruptcy filing to qualify for a cramdown under Chapter 13.
2. If the 910-day rule is met, the car loan can be reduced to the vehicle's current market value, lowering the secured debt you must pay.
3. Any remaining loan balance above the car's value becomes unsecured debt, which often receives little or no payment in a Chapter 13 plan.

4. Cramdowns cannot be used on purchase-money auto loans bought within 910 days, regardless of financial hardship or lender agreement.

5. The interest rate on the car loan can be reduced during the cramdown, further lowering monthly payments under the plan.

6. Cramdowns directly lower Chapter 13 plan payments, because secured debt and its interest rate heavily influence the plan's monthly base.

7. A motion to modify the plan is required, and the court must approve the cramdown before the reduced loan terms become binding.

8. Credible vehicle valuation is essential, typically through appraisals, NADA or KBB data, or dealer offers, to prove the car's true market value.

9. The lender may object, but objections cannot override eligibility—if the 910 rule is satisfied and proof is solid, the cramdown can move forward.

10. Once approved, the modified plan replaces the original, requiring the debtor to follow the new secured payment amount, interest rate, and updated plan base.

Chapter 16

Dismissal: The Final Step to End Your Chapter 13 Payments

When you file for Chapter 13 bankruptcy, you commit to the process. You complete the required financial courses, attend every hearing, and make your trustee payments month after month. The mission seems simple: stay the course, finish your plan, and avoid dismissal at all costs.

But here's the twist most people never see coming: there are rare—but very real—moments when seeking dismissal is actually the smart move.

Yes, you read that correctly.

You can voluntarily request to dismiss your Chapter 13 case, and in some situations, doing so can free you from the burden of ongoing plan payments. Whether your financial picture has changed, a better strategy has emerged, or your original goals no longer make sense, dismissal can become a strategic "exit door" built directly into the Bankruptcy Code.

This isn't a tool you pull out often. In fact, it's one of the last options on the table. But when used at the right time—and for the right reasons—it becomes a powerful way to take back control.

In this chapter, we'll break down exactly how dismissal works, why it exists, and how you can use it to your advantage when every other path has been exhausted.

Discharge vs. Dismissal

Bankruptcy attorney Reed Allmand explains that discharge and dismissal are "two different actions."

- **Discharge**: The ideal outcome in a Chapter 13 case. Completing your plan successfully and paying the required portion of your unsecured debts leads to a discharge. You are no longer legally responsible for those debts, and creditors can no longer pursue collection.
- **Dismissal**: Ends the case with very different consequences. Your debts remain, creditors may resume collection—including foreclosure or repossession—and you essentially return to your pre-bankruptcy situation.

When the consequences are manageable, strategic dismissal can be used to end your plan payments and close out Chapter 13 on your own terms.

Dismissal: Voluntary vs. Involuntary

Chapter 13 cases can be dismissed in two ways: **voluntarily by the debtor** or **involuntarily by the court**.

Voluntary Dismissal

A voluntary dismissal is when *you* choose to end your case. Under 11 U.S.C. § 1307(b), you have the right to dismiss your Chapter 13 case *at any time*—so long as it has not been converted to Chapter 7:

"On request of the debtor *at any time*, if the case has not been converted... the court shall dismiss a case under this chapter. Any waiver of the right to dismiss... is unenforceable."

This means no creditor, trustee, or judge can force you to remain in Chapter 13.

Example:

Jennifer files Chapter 13 to reorganize her debts. A few months later, she receives a substantial pay raise and an unexpected inheritance. With her improved finances, she decides she no longer needs bankruptcy protection. She consults her attorney and files a motion for voluntary dismissal. With no objections, the court grants her request. Jennifer's case ends, and she is no longer required to make payments under the bankruptcy plan, though her debts remain her responsibility.

Involuntary Dismissal

An involuntary dismissal occurs when the court ends your case, usually because you failed to comply with Chapter 13 rules. This can be triggered by a creditor, the trustee, or the court itself.

Common reasons include missed payments, failure to file required documents, or failure to follow court orders.

Under 11 U.S.C. § 1307(c):

"The court may dismiss a case under this chapter, whichever is in the best interests of creditors and the estate, for cause..."

Example:

John files Chapter 13 and is required to make $500 monthly plan payments. After several months, he misses multiple payments and does not catch up. The trustee files a motion to dismiss for nonpayment. After review, the court dismisses the case.

Whether voluntary or involuntary, the end result is the same: your Chapter 13 case is over, and your plan payments stop immediately.

Most Common Reasons for an Involuntary Dismissal

Chapter 13 has many requirements, often with strict deadlines. Failing to comply with any of these can lead to involuntary dismissal. Common causes include:

1. **Failure to Make Plan Payments** – Regular payments to the trustee are essential. Missing payments without efforts to catch up can trigger dismissal.

2. **Failure to File Required Forms** – All required forms must be submitted on time. Missing deadlines can result in dismissal.

3. **Failure to Disclose All Income** – Omitting household income, once discovered, can lead to dismissal.

4. **Failure to Attend Mandatory Hearings** – Missing key hearings like the creditors' meeting or plan confirmation may result in dismissal.

5. **Failure to Provide Information for Confirmation** – Not supplying your attorney with necessary documents can trigger dismissal.

6. **Fraud** – Hiding assets, debts, or income, or providing false information under penalty of perjury, results in dismissal.

7. **Failure to Complete Pre-Bankruptcy Credit Counseling** – Completion of an approved course within 180 days prior to filing is required. Failure may lead to dismissal.

8. **Failure to Pay the Court Filing Fee** – Fees must be paid or an approved installment plan requested. Nonpayment can lead to dismissal.

9. **Failure to Pay Monthly Child Support** – Child support obligations must continue during your case. Nonpayment may result in dismissal.

10. **Failure to File a Plan** – Your repayment plan must be filed and approved. Delays or missing documents can trigger dismissal.

Regardless of the reason, the result is the same: your case is dismissed, and plan payments stop.

STEP-BY-STEP GUIDE: Using Dismissal to End Plan Payments

Step 1: Evaluate Your Case

Before taking extreme action, assess whether alternatives exist to resolve issues with your plan payments. If no options remain, dismissal may be the final approach.

Step 2: Weigh Your Options

There are two types of dismissal—voluntary and involuntary. Dismissal is a serious measure, and many attorneys may not recommend it unless necessary. Consider the consequences carefully.

Step 3: Consult Your Attorney

Always discuss your case with your attorney. They can explain the full impact of dismissal, including consequences for your debts and creditors. If both of you agree, proceed to the next step.

Step 4: Proceed with Dismissal

- **Voluntary dismissal:** File a motion to dismiss your Chapter 13 case with the court. Forms and guidance are available on the U.S. Trustee website.
- **Involuntary dismissal:** Noncompliance with bankruptcy requirements—like failing to provide documents or make payments—can trigger dismissal by the court.

Regardless of method, the case ends once the court approves dismissal, and all plan payments cease.

Step 5: End Your Plan Payments

Once the court enters the dismissal order as noted, payments to the trustee stop immediately. Dismissal and plan payments are directly linked: end the case, and the payments end with it.

10 Key Points

1. A dismissal can be used strategically to end your Chapter 13 case and eliminate plan payments.
2. Chapter 13 dismissals can be voluntary (initiated by the debtor) or involuntary (initiated by the court for noncompliance).
3. A debtor has the right to request dismissal at any time, unless the case has been converted.
4. Any waiver of the right to dismiss a Chapter 13 case is unenforceable.
5. A dismissal is different from a discharge.
6. A discharge removes the legal obligation to pay debts, but a dismissal leaves debts intact.
7. Once a case is dismissed, the automatic stay is immediately lifted.
8. Creditors may resume collection efforts after dismissal.
9. Voluntary dismissal allows a debtor to exit bankruptcy on their own terms.
10. Involuntary dismissal occurs when the court ends the case due to noncompliance.

BANKRUPTCY GLOSSARY

A

11 U.S.C. § 1307(b)

The Bankruptcy Code provision giving a debtor the absolute right to voluntarily dismiss a Chapter 13 case, provided it has not been previously converted.

11 U.S.C. § 1307(c)

The Bankruptcy Code provision allowing the court to involuntarily dismiss a Chapter 13 case for cause, such as missed plan payments or noncompliance.

11 U.S.C. § 1329

The Bankruptcy Code section governing how a confirmed Chapter 13 plan may be modified after confirmation.

341 Meeting (Meeting of Creditors)

A mandatory hearing where the trustee verifies the debtor's identity, reviews the bankruptcy documents, and may ask questions about finances and the plan. Creditors may attend but usually do not. It also establishes certain deadlines, including claim-filing dates.

910-Day Rule

A bankruptcy rule prohibiting cramdowns on purchase-money vehicle loans when the vehicle was bought within 910 days (about 2.5 years) of filing Chapter 13.

Above-Median Debtor

A debtor whose household income exceeds the state median, generally requiring a 60-month Chapter 13 plan.

Affidavit / Declaration

A sworn written statement used to support motions such as a hardship discharge.

Applicable Commitment Period (ACP)

The required length of a Chapter 13 plan—typically 36 months for below-median debtors and 60 months for above-median debtors.

Appraisal

A documented estimate of a vehicle's current market value used during cramdown litigation.

Asset Liquidation (Chapter 7)

The process where a Chapter 7 trustee may sell nonexempt property to pay creditors.

Assets

Anything the debtor owns that must be disclosed in the bankruptcy schedules, including real estate, vehicles, cash, tools, and personal property.

Automatic Stay

A federal court protection that immediately stops collections, lawsuits, repossessions, and garnishments after filing bankruptcy. It ends if the case is dismissed.

B

BAPCPA (Bankruptcy Abuse Prevention and Consumer Protection Act of 2005)

Legislation that added major restrictions to bankruptcy practice, including the means test and the 910-day rule.

Bankruptcy Code

The federal statutes governing all bankruptcy cases.

Bankruptcy Discharge

A court order that permanently eliminates the debtor's personal liability for certain debts.

Bankruptcy Petition

The legal document filed to start a bankruptcy case, including required forms, schedules, and statements.

Bar Date

The strict deadline for creditors to file a Proof of Claim (POC).

Bar Date Notice

The notice informing creditors of the deadline to file a POC.

Best Effort Requirement

The requirement that a debtor devote all disposable income to unsecured creditors during the plan.

Beyond the Debtor's Control

A hardship discharge requirement showing that the event causing payment failure was unforeseen and unavoidable.

Binding Effect of Confirmation

Once a Chapter 13 plan is confirmed, both the debtor and creditors must follow its terms.

C

Case Dismissal

Termination of a Chapter 13 case due to failure to comply with plan or court requirements.

Certificate of Service

Proof that required parties received notice of a motion or legal filing.

Chapter 7 Bankruptcy

A liquidation bankruptcy that eliminates unsecured debts, usually without requiring monthly payments.

Chapter 7 Liquidation Test

A test comparing what unsecured creditors would receive in Chapter 7 to what they receive in Chapter 13.

Chapter 13 Bankruptcy

A repayment bankruptcy where the debtor pays into a court-approved plan for 3–5 years.

Chapter 13 Case Dismissal

Termination of a case—voluntarily by the debtor or involuntarily by the court.

Chapter 13 Plan

A detailed proposal describing how the debtor will pay creditors over 3–5 years.

Chapter 13 Plan Payment

The monthly payment made to the Chapter 13 trustee under the confirmed plan.

Chapter 13 Trustee

The court-appointed official who reviews documents, conducts the 341 meeting, collects payments, and distributes money to creditors.

Claim

A creditor's right to payment in bankruptcy.

Confirmed Plan

The repayment plan approved by the judge that binds both debtor and creditors.

Conversion (Chapter 13 to Chapter 7)

The legal process of switching a case from Chapter 13 to Chapter 7.

Creditor

Any person or entity the debtor owes money to.

Creditor Distribution

The trustee's payment of funds to creditors under the plan.

Creditor Objection

A formal filing opposing a plan, modification, or motion.

Creditor Registry

A trustee-prepared report listing all filed claims and their status.

Creditor Standing

A creditor's legal ability to file or enforce a claim.

Cramdown

A tool allowing a debtor to reduce an auto loan's secured amount to the vehicle's market value.

Cramdown Interest Rate

A court-approved interest rate applied to the reduced secured portion of a cramdown loan.

D

Debt Discharge

The elimination of qualifying debts after completing the bankruptcy process.

Debt Structure

How debts are categorized—secured, priority, and unsecured.

Disposable Income

Income remaining after deducting necessary living expenses, used to determine plan payments.

Distribution

Payments made by the trustee to creditors based on allowed claims.

Disallowed Claim

A claim rejected by the court due to errors, lateness, or insufficient proof.

Dismissal

Termination of a case before completion; does not eliminate debts.

Dollar-for-Dollar Reduction

The principle that disallowed claims reduce the plan's repayment obligation by the exact amount of the claim.

Documentation Requirement (Rule 3001(c)(1))

A rule requiring creditors to attach supporting documents (contracts, statements) to their POC.

Documentation / Proof of Lost Income

Evidence such as pay stubs or termination letters used to justify modification.

E

Evidence Packet

Supporting documents submitted with a motion, such as a hardship discharge.

Executory Contracts

Contracts where both parties still have obligations, such as leases.

Exemptions (Bankruptcy Exemptions)

Laws protecting certain property from liquidation.

Exhibit

A numbered document attached to a motion.

Extend the Plan / Plan Extension

A plan modification increasing the repayment period up to the 60-month maximum.

F

Feasibility

A requirement that the plan is affordable based on income and expenses.

Financial Hardship

A significant decrease in income or resources making plan payments unmanageable.

Financial Rehabilitation

The goal of Chapter 13—to reorganize debts and achieve long-term stability.

G

General Unsecured Creditor

A creditor with no collateral securing the debt.

Good Faith

A requirement that filings and modifications be made honestly and fairly.

H

Hanging Paragraph

An unnumbered sentence after §1325(a)(9) that restricts cramdowns on recently purchased vehicles.

Hardship Discharge

An early discharge granted when a debtor cannot complete plan payments due to circumstances beyond their control and meeting three legal requirements.

Hearing

A court session where motions, objections, or modifications are decided.

Household Contributions

Money from family members used to assist with expenses or plan payments.

I

Income

All money received by the debtor, including wages, business income, benefits, and contributions.

Income Changes

Any increase or decrease in income that affects plan feasibility.

Informal Adjustment

A payment change negotiated with the trustee without immediate court filing.

Involuntary Dismissal

A dismissal initiated by the court for cause.

IRS National and Local Standards

Standardized expense guidelines used in the means test.

J

Job Loss

Loss of employment that may justify modifying plan payments.

L

Late-Filed Claim

A Proof of Claim submitted after the bar date, typically disallowed.

Legal Minimum Payment

The lowest payment amount the Bankruptcy Code allows in a plan.

Linchpin (Chapter 13 Modification)

The essential mechanism—§1329 modification—that enables lowering plan payments.

Living Expenses

Ordinary costs of living used to calculate disposable income.

M

Market Value (Car Value)

The current value of a vehicle used in cramdown calculations.

Means Test

A tool measuring income against expenses to determine plan length and feasibility.

Median Income

The income benchmark used in the means test.

Meeting of Creditors

See: 341 Meeting.

Modification (Plan Modification)

A court-approved change to the Chapter 13 plan.

Modified Plan

The revised version of the plan submitted after financial changes.

Monthly Plan Payment

The amount due each month to the trustee.

Motion

A written request asking the court to take an action.

Motion for Hardship Discharge

A request asking the court to end the plan early due to hardship.

Motion to Convert / Notice of Conversion

The filing that formally switches a case to Chapter 7.

Motion to Modify

A filing requesting court approval to change a confirmed plan.

N

Net Income Statement

A document showing income minus expenses.

No-Asset Case

A Chapter 7 case where no nonexempt property is available for liquidation.

Noncompliance

Failure to follow bankruptcy rules or orders.

Nonexempt Property

Assets that may be sold in Chapter 7.

Nonpriority Unsecured Debt

Unsecured debts that do not receive special priority.

O

Objection

A challenge to a claim, motion, discharge request, or modification.

P

Payment Adjustment

A change in monthly payments reflecting new circumstances.

Payment Duration

The length of time plan payments must be made.

Payment Reduction

A decrease in required monthly payments.

Payment Schedule

The timetable for making plan payments.

Petition Package

All documents required to file a bankruptcy case.

Plan Base

The total amount the debtor must pay into the plan.

Plan Duration / Repayment Period

The total length of the plan—typically 36 to 60 months.

Plan Modification Motion

A motion requesting that the court approve changes to plan terms.

Plan Payments

Monthly payments made to the trustee.

Priority Debt

Debts that must be paid in full, such as taxes or child support.

Priority/Discretionary Expenses

Allowed expenses deducted to determine disposable income.

Proof of Claim (POC)

A required document creditors file to participate in payment.

Purchase-Money Auto Loan

A car loan used specifically to buy the vehicle.

R

Reasonable Living Expenses

Necessary household expenses used to calculate disposable income.

Reaffirmation Agreement

A voluntary agreement to continue paying a secured debt after conversion to Chapter 7.

Reclassification

Dividing a loan into secured and unsecured portions during a cramdown.

Regular Source of Income

Any stable income used to fund a Chapter 13 plan.

Reorganization Plan

Another term for the Chapter 13 plan.

S

Schedules

Official forms listing assets, debts, income, expenses, and financial history.

Secured Claim / Secured Debt

A debt backed by collateral.

Service of Process

Formal delivery of legal documents to required parties.

Shortfall

When secured and priority debts exceed disposable income.

Significant Change in Circumstances

A major financial shift requiring plan modification.

Statement of Financial Affairs

A document listing the debtor's financial history.

Supporting Documentation

Evidence attached to a POC or motion.

Supporting Declaration

A sworn statement explaining hardship or income changes.

Surrender

Returning collateral to the creditor voluntarily.

T

Total Repayment Amount

The amount that must be paid into the plan.

Trustee

A court-appointed official handling payments, claims, and administration.

Trustee Review

The trustee's evaluation of a modification or claim.

TRCC (Trustee's Recommendation Concerning Claims)

A report evaluating all filed claims and recommending which should be allowed or disallowed.

Trustee's Fee

A percentage deducted from plan payments for administrative costs.

U

U.S. Trustee

A federal official overseeing bankruptcy cases in each district.

Under-Mcdian Debtor

A debtor earning less than the state median, eligible for a 36-month plan.

Unexpired Leases

Leases still active at the time of filing.

Unforeseen Economic Circumstances

Unexpected events such as job loss or illness supporting hardship discharge requests.

Unsecured Creditor / Unsecured Debt

A creditor whose debt is not backed by collateral.

Updated Schedules (I & J)

Revised income and expense schedules filed after conversion or major changes.

Voluntary Dismissal

When a debtor chooses to end a Chapter 13 case.

Voluntary Petition

The official form that begins a bankruptcy case when filed.